Miracles Galor---ious

To Emma Grace —
You are such a blessing
May Be Blessed
with —
Miracles Galor---ious
Rwonda Baker
3/9/19

Miracles Galor---ious

Revonda Zubiena Boykin

Heavenly
Light Press
Alpharetta, GA

ISBN: 978-1-63183-494-3 - Paperback

Printed in the United States of America   0 2 1 8 1 9

⊗This paper meets the requirements of ANSI/NISO Z39.48-1992 (Permanence of Paper)

All scripture quotations are taken from the Holy Bible, King James Version (Public Domain).

As I wrote this account of my many miracles and blessings, I was approached by my granddaughter, Emma. She wanted to know if I would maybe come to her school and share about my book with her class. There was so much pride in her voice as she looked at me with her request.

"Of course, I will," I replied. She then asked if I would read some of the stories to her. As I watched and read, she was so thrilled, and immediately gave her approval to the stories.

After reading and giving her most respectable comment, she asked, "Meemaw, can I have a copy for my very own?"

You can just imagine what that meant to me. I told her, "Not only will I give you your own copy, but I will dedicate my book to you."

A broad grin adorned her precious face as in disbelief she exclaimed, "Really?" and I proudly said, "Really."

For her faith, love, and extreme courage through a most difficult time in her very young life, I do indeed dedicate my book of miracles to Emma. May she continue to grow in wisdom, statue, and favor with both God and all she meets here on this earth. She is a special child of God. I love her dearly, and it is my prayer that she, too, will be blessed with *Miracles Galor---ious*.

Contents

Acknowledgments...ix

Introduction xi

He's an On-Time God 1

Mull and the Car Wreck... 6

Angel on the Highway... 9

Who Was Driving the Car? 12

The Rusty Nail..15

Scot's Campfire 18

Dear God, It's Cathy 21

Ka-plunk! 23

Small Miracles of Joy 27

The Christmas Card..30

Scot's Fishing Trip..32

Jay Jay, the Boy Who Wouldn't...37

An Issue of Blood 43

A Child to Love 45

The Pancake Mix 50

Joyce's Rooster...56

Death Jump..60

Pride and Joy 65

Miracle on the Highway..68

Ryan, the Rescue Hero 73

Translation Peace 77

My God Is My Carpenter 80

A Most Magnificent Stove..83

God Provided Our Home 86

He Is Going to Breathe 89

Miracle of Sight 94

Lord, My Car's in My Garden 101

The Pink Mountain 106

Red Light, Green Light..108

The Last Whoop 112

Winter Wonderland 116
Sophisticated Test 119
The Motorcycle Crash...123
Who Was on the Swing? 126
Angel Unaware 130
God's Minute Helicopter...133
Gift of God's Love...135
A Very Definite Healing Miracle...137
Return to Grace 139
A Very Unprecedented Pie 141
God at Work 144
A Rough Cut..147
He Is at Peace . . . Wrong! 149
The Blessed Vision 151
A Most Precious Soul..153
Confident 159
Don't Use That Saw! 162
The Rose..164

Acknowledgments

First and foremost, I am grateful and wish to sincerely thank all of my family members: my daughter Kelli, who insisted that Mama write these so as not to lose them to her and her family; to my daughter Jenna, who together with her children supplied some of these miracle stories; to my son, Scot, who never let there be a dull moment in my life.

A special thanks to Ryan for his assistance in all operational matters. May the Lord truly bless him for his efforts.

Most of all, I want to thank my grandson, Cory, without whom I could not have gotten this done. He was my encouragement, and along with his mom, my most constructive critic. For Ryan, who has been with me throughout the entire publishing process. For Eric and Daniel, who assisted me with the trials of technology. Last and most important, my God, who generously supplied the miracles in my life.

Introduction

Over the years I have basked in the blessing of many miracles in my life. When I was anointed to teach, I told the Lord that I was an empty vessel, to which the Lord replied, "You are a good storyteller." The miracles became background for the lessons and became something of pleasure to those I taught.

Many people have told me to write these down and not to forget them, because they would be such a blessing to my children and grandchildren, and others who could share in God's glorious works. It was because of these people that I decided to put together some of the miracles that God had given me, and attempt to show a correlation to similar incidents for others today.

Too often, I feel people do not realize a miracle has happened, or that they are on the brink of a miracle happening and miss it completely.

- That day when it is raining very hard, and you get to the store with no time to wait for the rain to stop, you realize you forgot your umbrella. You open the car door to dash into the store, so as not to get too wet, and suddenly realize the rain has stopped just long enough for you to get inside.
- You need a special gift for someone and find it in the back of the shelf: the last one.
- Then, an icy road, and the people in front of you slam on their brakes. You slide into the car in front, not marring their car and only minor damage to yours, and later find it amazingly repaired.
- You have no food, but suddenly find something you did not know you had.
- The test results show your possible diagnosis to be negative.
- You need a parking place, and under your breath, say, "Lord, help me find a parking place," and suddenly there is one right in front of where you are going.

These are not coincidences; they are *miracles* from a Holy God who provides for us from His bounty.

With this collection of blessings, I hope to show that anyone who believes can and will experience miracles, if only they will trust in the One who gives them so generously to us.

I want to thank my God, who supplied me with all the wonderful blessings beyond my fondest dreams. To Him be the Glory.

He's an On-Time God

"Likewise, I say unto you, there is joy in the presence of the angels of God over one sinner that repenteth."
—Luke 15:10

I feel it necessary to begin these accounts with the most significant miracle of all: salvation, which comes from the Most Mighty One of all, Jesus. The miracle of His power and His majesty, sovereignty, and His love for me are beyond anything I could imagine. Without Him, I would be lost in a world of tragedy, disillusion, hopelessness, and fear. He has chosen to love me in spite of my ugliness, and to completely wipe from his remembrance all the sin I have thoughtlessly committed against Him. He has said He will spread it as far as east is from west, and as high as the heavens and deep as the ocean, away from His thoughts forever. How wonderful can that be, and how miraculous for me? I praise Him, and bless Him, and love Him today and forever.

It was my great privilege to have family members share the miracle of my father's conversion. He had turned twenty-four years of age on February 27, 1940. I was only three years old, about to become four in October. My dad came from a devoted family, where he knew his father and mother to be godly people. My grandfather was the superintendent of Sunday school at their church, sang in the choir, served on the board of elders, and walked the Christian walk every day of his life. My granny, like so, was a godly woman. She started each day with her Bible reading and prayer, and was one of the charter members of Maple Avenue Church.

So, Dad grew up seeing this behavior and commitment to the Lord all his life. His sister, who was three years older than he, stood in this teaching and received it all of her life. This was an exceptional home of Christian values which were practiced at all times. It was a home where others were invited in on Sunday for meals, and good talk, and sharing of God's word. It was a home of outgrowth to the community service and those who were less fortunate. This was the best of the best, as for homes. There was soft talk, and hopeful dreams, and prosperity spoken always.

1

Though he had had all the training a child should have in his home, he had never personally received Jesus as his savior. My mother was not a Christian, and had not been brought up in this kind of home. It was not really the will of my granny and grandpa that Daddy marry my mother, but he chose her. She was the only one for him, and that was that. Church was not a part of their life, apart or together, and this was of great concern to my grandparents. They never stopped praying for my dad that God would bring to his memory all the things of his youth, and that someday he would want the life he had known so well.

Though he was an obedient son in all ways, the parting of the road came with good times, fun, and excitement. These were the kinds of things Mother and her family lived. Good and respectable people, pillars of the community, but not necessarily godly people. He had done well in school and was well thought of by the school teachers and classmates. Lee was fun, happy, personable, but he was lost. In his state, the hope of Heaven was just not a priority for him. Ultimately, the two were married and planned their family.

He dearly loved his wife; she was his soul mate. He called her "doll," and idolized her as his most precious sweetheart. He was thrilled when children came: first me, and then my sister. However, he really longed for a son. He loved fishing, and hunting, and wood carving, and all the things that a man would enjoy, and wanted to share this with a son, as his dad had done with him. He followed in his father's footsteps with woodworking, and was employed in the factory where the famous Brumby Rockers were manufactured. In those days, few people had cars. All worked near their home and walked to and from. So was the case with my daddy.

It was one of those hot summer days when walking to and from work was difficult. The heat was extreme and draining, especially after working in the factory. Today, he felt tired, but as he passed by the little church on Maple Avenue, he saw on the directory that a revival would be starting tonight. As he proceeded in his walk, he stopped by his family home to get a good drink of water. The house was located on Poplar Street, and this was on his way home, so he often stopped off for a few minutes to chat with his mom.

The large house was the largest on the street, and certainly the most beautiful of any. It was big with a nice lot surrounded by privet hedges, which Grandpa prided himself to keep blocked to make a fence across the front of the property. Granny had planted large weigela of several different degrees of pink in the yard, and had a floral garden at the side with marigold, bachelor buttons, daisies, and iris—always beautiful.

There was a great front porch with a swing that Grandpa made. He also had made shelves on top of the bannisters to hold many pots of ferns and other plants, and certainly six Brumby Rockers enhanced the area, where many neighbors came to sit.

It was this day when Dad came by and went to the back porch, where a well was located. He lowered the bucket that was there, and while talking to his mom, drew up the cool, wonderful water, for which he had come to enjoy. Granny asked, "Will you come to church tonight? Preacher Hampton will be preaching."

Daddy responded, "I don't know, but I'll think about it."

Granny continued to talk about the service and that she really wanted him to come. He loved his mom very much, always wanting to please her. He finally agreed he would be there, finished his water from the dipper that always stayed in the bucket, and went on his way.

The little church was ready for the service. The handheld funeral-home fans were appropriately scattered, the lean-out stained-glass windows were pushed out, and all was ready for the service. It was almost time, approximately 7:00 p.m., when the people started to arrive. Granny looked at each person as they came into the church, and it began to fill up. Dad was not there.

Time for the music to start. Aunt Edith, my dad's sister, was the piano player, and so started the old, well-known hymns. "Come to the Church in the Wildwood" seemed to always start the service, then "I Come to the Garden Alone," "Old Rugged Cross," and more. Granny never turned around again, almost not really wanting to see the pews, lest she had to realize her son was not there.

As the preaching started, Preacher Hampton talked about forgiveness and the necessity of being redeemed, and finally gave the altar call and invitation. It appeared there would be no conversions tonight. As the song of invitation played, Preacher Hampton seemingly begged for someone to come forward. No one came. In frustration, the large, humble man came down off the pulpit area to the floor space in front. He proclaimed, "God says there is one here who does not have the assurance of tomorrow. This person does not realize his destiny is at hand. Won't you come now? Come, come!"

The music started again. No move. No one saw my daddy, who had slipped in the door at the last minute and took residence to the back row. Now standing, he was holding onto the pew in front of him. His knuckles were white from holding on so tightly, hoping he could hang on and not move at all.

Preacher Hampton would not be dissuaded, not tonight. God had placed the desire for one soul in his heart, and he would not give up. Daddy would hang on tighter, his heart pounding in his chest, almost up and in his throat now. Feeling almost faint, his worst nightmare happened. Preacher Hampton began to walk down the aisle. With his arm raised and moving back and forth, he searched for that soul. He came nearer and nearer. Daddy almost ran out the door, but he was captive now. All eyes were turned to Preacher Hampton, and this was in direct line with my daddy.

Dad began to shake. He knew what was coming. Hopefully the preacher would turn around and go back to the front, but this did not happen. Then, that gentle, determined man came to the row where Daddy stood, stopped, and pointed, and in a soft, yet stern voice, he said, "God is calling you, son. Don't let him down. Step out. Come on, boy. God wants you."

With that, my daddy turned loose of the pew. His hands were now wet with sweat. His head was wet, and with tearful eyes, he ran to the altar and fell on it there. Immediately, my granny and grandpa were at his side, and he gave his heart to Jesus and received the victorious gift of salvation.

All those prayers had finally paid off! My granny was elated, and the church body was thrilled. They, too, had joined my granny in her prayers for my daddy. Now, those prayers were answered. Miracle, yes, but none knew just how significant it was.

Less than thirty days after this wonderful thing happened, once again my daddy left the factory, walking home. He passed by the little church and paused for a moment, remembering that night when all his burdens were lifted, when he was "washed in the blood of the lamb." He said a quiet prayer of thanks to his Master and went on his way.

As usual, he stopped to lower the bucket on the back porch again into the well for a cool drink of water, and chat with small talk about his day with his mom and sister, and was on his way. They asked if he would stay for a bite to eat, but he said that Doll would have dinner ready, so he would go on. He noted that he felt unusually tired today and had a slight headache. Saying goodbye and giving a hug to his mom, he left.

He walked up Poplar to Polk, and then progressed on to Powder Springs Street, cutting across Atlanta Street, and finally to Frazure Street and up the hill to their little home on the back of the property of the well-known General Clay. As he approached the house, he could smell the aroma of the meal Doll had prepared for him. He knew that when he walked in the door, she would put the biscuits in the stove and he would go wash up.

Today, he called to her and said, "Don't put the biscuits in yet! I really need to cool off a bit. Why don't you take the kids for a walk and let me have a little nap?"

Mother said, "I have already fed the children, so that would be good. Maybe they will go to sleep early and we can have some quiet time together."

Daddy was pleased with that, and he went in, washed up, and crawled onto the bed for a rest.

Mother took us in the stroller and we walked over to see a neighbor. As Mother was talking and I was jumping up and down on the small wall I wanted to walk on, my little sister, Joyce, now only twenty-one months old, went to sleep. Mother was holding her in her arms and felt that Joyce had wet her diaper. So, after approximately thirty minutes, she chose to return to the house to change Joyce's diaper.

As we entered the house, my Uncle "Bug," who had been out on the tennis court behind the house, came around and picked me up, and took me into the house. I wanted some water, so Bug took me to the kitchen. We had one of those cabinets that was freestanding and had a pull-out, porcelain, shelf-like top on it, and Bug placed me there to get a glass out and get my water.

There was a sudden frantic scream from my mother. Bug dropped the glass and ran, leaving me on the cabinet. Mother was screaming, "Lee is dead! Lee is dead!"

My daddy, twenty-four years of age, was indeed dead. He had suffered a stroke, and was gone. I recall the trauma to everyone we knew. Such a shock . . . so young, so vital, and now, so dead.

The significance of the miracle became very real to everyone. Ira Lee Gregg became the newest resident of Heaven that day.

Praise God, Preacher Hampton did not give up. Praise God, Daddy was obedient to God, and Praise God, he was redeemed and washed whiter than snow. I was protected. I would, in my life, also be claimed by that Mighty God.

The miracle of salvation took a while, but God knew the time. God was on the throne, and God was the Mighty God and Savior of all. There was exceeding joy in Heaven that day; all the angels were rejoicing. Though the family was devastated, they, too, had the joy of knowing that my daddy was in Heaven, and they would one day see him again.

It is my sincere belief that when my dad was taken to Heaven, that God Himself took on that role of "daddy" for me. He has always been there, during my childhood and now, and is just as real to me as my Heavenly Father today. Jesus bore it all, and all to Him I vow, to Him be the glory. My God is always on time: not one minute too early or too late—just in time. He is indeed "an on-time God."

And the angels rejoiced over another soul claimed for Jesus.

Mull and the Car Wreck

"Be not afraid of sudden fear, neither of desolation of the wicked, when it cometh. For the Lord shall be thy confidence, and shall keep thy foot from being taken."
—Proverbs 3:25, 26

It seems that my life has always had many miracles. Understanding these and why I have been so blessed is a mystery, to say the least. I believe that when you pray about something, and a response to that prayer happens, this is indeed a miracle afforded from our Lord.

I have been trying to remember when the first miracle I recognized to be such happened in my life. Certainly, my protection from many dangers would come to mind, but then there were those which were really miraculous blessings. Nevertheless, still miracles.

One of the first stories of my memory was a time during World War II, when all the young men were taken to war. Many women and children, as were we, were left at home to fend for themselves. This was the case with my family.

My father had passed away at the young age of twenty-four years old. He suffered from rheumatic fever, which caused damage to his heart, which was the source of the stroke that took his young life. My mother was left with two little girls, one three years old and the other twenty-one months old. Since Social Security had just come on the scene, only one payment had been made by my dad. No benefits were available for Mother to access for our support. This meant she would have to go to work.

My grandmother was the caregiver for my grandfather, who suffered from Parkinson's disease and was bedridden. He was a veteran of the Spanish-American War, and had a pension from that. Otherwise, no income would have been there for my grandmother, either. Because of all the women and children left behind, Mama, which we called my grandmother, suggested we all come together and move in with her. This was decided so that we could protect one another.

Therefore, a rented, large colonial home was chosen. It had many bedrooms and bathrooms, and was centrally located within walking distance to the downtown area. This was a good thing, as we shared tokens and stamps necessary to purchase food items. With all of us living together, we had plenty of milk, sugar, and other necessary items. Mother worked outside the home and contributed her fair share, as did my Uncle James. James did not qualify for the enlistment. Therefore, he was the man of the house.

The house was on a busy street, the main one leading from Marietta to Atlanta. There were streetcars which passed regularly, this being the means of commuting to and from work. Few people had their own personal vehicles. The house was on a corner lot with approximately one or two acres of yard, so it appeared safe for us children to play outside. These were the calm days, with easygoing lifestyles by most. We sat and listened to the radio, visited with neighbors, and certainly neighbors came over to sit on the large porch. The ladies knitted and crocheted socks for servicemen and talked about the war.

In the front yard was a wide walkway leading to the steps to the porch and large oak trees on the grassy lawn. On the right side of the walkway was a dogwood tree that we children liked to build our playhouse under. We would sweep the dirt away from squares and line the squares with the swept-up dirt to make bedrooms, living rooms, etc. This outlined our house. We used rocks to outline our sofas, beds, etc., and gathered weeds and leaves to pretend cooking.

Today was again as most days. We had our dolls, some dishes, some pieces of cloth, and began making our playhouse, three little girls being mommies with their dolls and playing "Let's Pretend." We had picked some leaves, some ragweed, and other things to put in our pot to make soup. We just about had our "dinner" completed when my aunt came and urged us to come in. She had made us some lemonade, cookies, and small sandwiches for lunch. We argued a little, but she was adamant we must come right now.

"Hurry, hurry," she said. Her voice was so strong and determined that we ran into the house and onto the screened porch off the back of the house. No sooner had we reached the back porch than came a screeching sound of skidding tires and breaking, then a large boom. A car had crashed into our house!

The police had been chasing a whiskey car, and the driver lost control. He veered off into our yard, crushing the side of the dogwood tree, and slammed into the side of the porch. The smell of the bootleg whiskey was very pungent, and the fear of the possibility of explosion was very real. The driver jumped and ran, and the police were running and chasing him down. He was eventually caught and taken to jail, and the car was carefully removed from the underspending of the porch.

As we came to observe the area, it became obvious that a miracle had occurred. The three of us little girls would certainly have been killed had we not moved immediately. The dolls, dishes, and other things with which we were playing were completely destroyed. This would certainly have been true of us three little girls.

When the smoke and odor cleared, we pondered what had occurred. My Aunt Ann gave her account: she said that as she was making the sandwiches, she suddenly became fearful and queasy in her stomach. She related that she felt the voice of an angel telling her to get us out of the yard quickly. She said she knew disaster was about to hit. She moved immediately to get us little ones in and as far away from the front as possible.

This is something I remember vividly, as if it happened yesterday. Everyone—with the exception of my cousin, Beverly, and I—have passed on to that other world, but we still are thankful and remember a miracle happened, because my aunt was obedient to heed the warning.

God gives us many warnings, often in just a feeling or a soft voice, but always, better to heed and it not be necessary than not to obey and suffer the consequences. Indeed, "For the Lord shall be our confidence, and keep our foot from being taken."

Praise be to the Lord.

Angel on the Highway

"Let your light so shine before men that they will see your good works and
glorify your Father, which is in Heaven."
—Matthew 5:16

Today, as I was about to climb out of my bed, I remembered times when I felt there had been the presence of angels experienced in my life. One of these times were when I was about nineteen years old and doing all those things that youngsters do that they should not. I had been involved in an accident previous to this time, certainly when I was spared.

My sister and I worked at Kennestone Hospital in Marietta, Georgia, on the night shift. This particular day as we left the hospital, we both laughed about being so tired, and without thinking said, "As tired as we are, don't be surprised if we come right back! We are too sleepy to drive."

Watch what you put into the air; it may come back to roost.

As we drove into what was then known as Pine Forest Apartments, where we lived, there was a large curve, and cars were parked on each side. This made the passage only large enough, really, for one car to pass, unless carefully being maneuvered. As we rounded the curve, another car coming the opposite was indeed not being cautious, and was pretty much in the middle of the road. We tried to dodge the head-on collision, and did, but also were crushed into a parked car on our side of the road. It was impossible for us to miss the other car, and a crash took place.

We were thrown into another parked car just before a large embankment and creek. Miraculously, we did not go over the embankment, but were injured. We recovered without residual injury and were blessed. After a long court battle, we received a settlement. With the settlement, I purchased my first car.

I bought a 1954 Mercury hardtop convertible. It was a pretty good car, but I wanted to really fix it up. So, with some of my money, I had it repainted a beautiful forest green with a "baby shoe" white top. It was very shiny and looked like new. I then proceeded to buy "baby shoe" white-leather seat covers, and boy, this was really snazzy.

I was proud of my car, but as with everything else in my life, I shared it a lot with other people, especially with my boyfriend and his friends, who were stationed at Dobbins AFB. It seemed that they kept it more than I did. I finally did wise up and stopped lending it out to everyone. It seemed no one else cared if it was kept clean or not. Then, I knew it was my car, not theirs, but you would think they would be more grateful for me sharing.

At this time, many of us were going to the NCO Club on Saturday and Sunday nights to dance to Kid Miller's band, and we all had a really good time. Most of us knew someone at the club and were able to get them to sign us in. This was one of those nights. I don't even remember all the particulars now; it was so many years ago, and has not crossed my mind in decades. I only know that someone made me very angry, and I ran out of the club.

The club was located at the end of the naval base runway and right off South Cobb Drive, or as we called it then, the "bomber-plant road." This was a long stretch of highway that ran in front of the parking lot of Lockheed Aircraft Company, and was more often than not a speedway. The highway was long and flat until you passed the portion of Lockheed, and then was right behind the fence to the air-force-base barracks. The "four lane," as it was then called, passed over an overpass, and the bomber-plant road went under the overpass. It also, when you kept right, went directly onto the four lane and onto the entrance of Dobbins AFB. Well, you get the picture, and as I scratched out of the parking lot and onto the highway, I was really going fast. The people who had upset me were right behind, trying to catch me, and that made me go that much faster. I was going, I am sure, at least 100 mph, trying to get away from my followers.

With teary eyes and so much anger I was not thinking straight, I suddenly was confused as to whether to go to the left fork or the right. Now too late, I took the middle. There was no road there, only a gravel space and an embankment that went over and off onto the road under the overpass. I immediately knew I was in trouble and tried to brake, but the gravel made me skid.

Suddenly, my car was suspended in air, until the wheels stopped turning and was put down. The rear wheels were on the edge of the embankment, and with just the lightest movement I would be over. My friends who had followed me and my boyfriend got out and jerked me out of the car. They were afraid it was going over the cliff.

I was shaking and traumatized by the actions, but shocked at what had just happened. No one could understand how I kept from going over the cliff or was able to stop, but I knew, because I felt the airborne status and then was gently put down.

It certainly would have taken more than one angel to stop and hold the car up like that. I had been spared again, and I knew God had a call on my life from that point on. It was time for me to show the God who was within me. I remembered our class motto at graduation, and I was led to live that motto: "Let your light so shine before men, that they may see your good works, and glorify your Father which is in heaven" (Matthew 5:16).

Who Was Driving the Car?

"And the ass saw the Angel of the Lord standing
in the way of the path, with his sword in his hand."
—Numbers 22:23

Angels play an important part in our lives, as directed by our Lord. At times we do not realize that they are present, but somehow, in the most dangerous of times, they suddenly appear and handle numerous situations, much to our protection.

I had not been graduated from high school very long when I went to work for the Arthur Murray Dance Studio. Here, I had met a very nice young man and dear friend. He had previously been stationed at the Dobbins AFB and decided to come to Atlanta to try to work for the dance studio. Having been a worker for the USO there on the base, I had previously met Frank. We became good friends, and later I introduced him to my roommate, with whom he started a relationship.

The summer was coming on and we were all excited to get to the beach, of course. Frank was on leave and had gone home to Florida, and since he and my roommate, Gloria, talked on the phone often, we decided to take the weekend and go see Frank. Also, he could ride back to the base with us and save him the price of a plane ticket. We also thought he would be great to help drive. Our heads were spinning about how to accomplish this trip and none of us get fired from our jobs.

Sara, my childhood friend, had just purchased her first car. It was a nice one: a Ford, four-door, roomy, and beautiful, as well. It was a light green and shined like new, although it was several years old. It had good tires, and had been checked out as to safety by her brother, and we were sure everything was okay. It was decided that we would leave right after getting off work on Friday and come back in time to go to work on Monday. Shorts, bathing suits, and all kinds of other things we just might need were thrown together. It was decided that Sara would start to drive, and when she got tired, Gloria would drive, and I would take the last shift.

This was before we had I-75 and good roads all the way. We had to travel Hwy

41, and then 141, and on south, mostly two-lane roads and nearly always in the view of the ocean whenever possible. These were lonely and dark roads with little or no places to stop. There were no rest areas at that time that I can remember, and gas stations were few and far between. We would fill up whenever we came across the gas station that was open. If there had been a rest area, they would have been dangerous, so we did not stop. We had packed a lunch and drinks in ice so as to be able to eat and drink at will, which we did. No air conditioning in the car, so all windows were down and our hair flying as we trudged on.

After a while, we knew it was time for a potty break, so we looked for a place that had rest rooms. As I recall, we had to ask for the key to get in, and they were certainly far from sanitary. But, relief we had, and with a few more snacks and more gas, we were on our way again.

Our first stop was Daytona Beach. We had called for reservations at a motel on the beach, where my family usually went on vacation, so they held the room for us. No sooner did we arrive than to the beach we went. Dark by then, but right on the beach, so we walked along in the water's edge and enjoyed the tide splashing against our legs, then decided to go in and eat again and sleep so as to get up early and play.

It was wonderful weather, and many other young people were at the beach also. Then, there was the famous boardwalk with the giant Ferris wheel and other rides. What a thrill to get on the great big wheel and go round and round, overlooking the ocean as far as we could possibly see! Occasionally, there were some porpoises jumping up and out of the water. What a beautiful sight! We rented some bikes to ride along the beach, and yes, meet boys from other areas to flirt with and plan to meet later. All day on Saturday we played and enjoyed sun and fun—until we came in and realized we were terribly sunburnt, that is.

Gloria got in touch with Frank and told him to expect us at his home no later than ten a.m. on Sunday. He advised that his family would be going to church, so we would have to find something to do until he was home. We agreed, and planned to leave no later than eleven p.m. to drive down to Miami.

So, we continued to enjoy the boardwalk, went to a dance place, and hung out for a while. Then it was getting late, so we loaded the car, checked out of the motel, and started to the Miami area, a long drive at night and not fully knowing where we were going. Sara was terribly sunburnt, so Gloria started the first round of driving. I stayed awake to help her navigate and watch for road signs, etc. We were so young and so irresponsible, we just wanted to have fun. Too much driving for a weekend, be we would get it all in . . . I guess.

About 150 to 200 miles in, Gloria expressed her extreme exhaustion and asked if I would drive. I knew I was just as tired and exhausted as she was, and Sara was sound asleep, so I agreed to take the wheel. We had driven another hundred miles, and I stopped for gas and to go to the rest room, and was refreshed somewhat. Everyone was awake for a while, and then we were back on that long, dark road.

I knew that I was very sleepy and had to keep washing my face with the ice-water bath cloth. I knew I was tired, but I did not realize that I was driving in "brain sleep" status. I just know that I suddenly hit a bump, and was off the side of the road. I was able to get back on, but something was strange. We were just entering the outskirts of Miami. The last time that I was aware, we were at least a hundred miles out. Somehow, we had gotten to our destination, but I could not remember driving it. Somehow, I had driven the car all that area essentially asleep! It was a bit frightening when I realized that I had been driving while sleeping, and that I had not only endangered my friends and myself, but every driver I must have encountered on the road.

"Who was driving the car?" I asked, and certainly I knew: once again, God had dispatched angels to watch over us girls. So young, so foolish, and so blessed to be safe. I am told that this happens more than anyone would possibly believe, but it does often lead to a disastrous end.

Going home, Frank was able to help drive and I was able to sleep, but even today, I am amazed that so many miles were driven while I was essentially asleep. Just as God sent the angels to stop Balaam, he also sent the angels to watch over us girls. This is a warning for other teens who think they are invincible. Just one bump could have lasting, terrible consequences.

I praise my God for being my Protector, and pray that this story will bring a new understanding to the importance of rest before traveling.

$\mathcal{T}$he Rusty Nail

"Jesus said unto him, If thou canst believe, all things are possible to him that believeth."
—Mark 9:23

It was in the latter part of May 1971 when my husband and I chose to move back to Georgia. We had moved to the St. Louis, Missouri, area for Richard to begin work at Chrysler Corporation. His dad was employed there and held a high position at the auto factory. We owned a home in Marietta, which had been leased for the time we were in St. Louis.

Upon arrival, we found a total mess. I began to plan renovations and clean up immediately. Our home was brand new when we left, and now it was in a shambles. The whole place seemed to have aged by ten years, and when I tried to put it back together, I realized what a job I had on my hands. I soon found that the bathroom floor was impossible to clean, and no amount of deodorizer seemed to take care of the odor. This had to be replaced.

Paint came first, then floors, then without any sense at all, I busted out the bathroom tile. We won't go into the problems I caused by doing this, but I learned a good lesson about "knowing what you are doing" before you do it. Next came window treatments and wallpaper, etc. While taking care of all of this, my aunt called and told me she was going to sell the sofa I had loved so much, and wondered if I would like to buy it. I did, indeed, but immediately decided to tear it up and reupholster it.

Richard just shook his head. For your information, my sister had been taking some classes in upholstery, so she agreed to assist me. First, I had to remove the old cover piece by piece, and label it so as to know where it went back, and then use these pieces to cut the new ones. I did the cushions first, since they had to be sewn and cording put in, and then proceeded to remove the other pieces of the sofa. All was going well . . . ha!

Joyce and I had had a discussion that morning about Jesus and His power. Joyce had accepted Christ as her savior, but was still a baby Christian. As we talked, I found that my sister did not know how to trust Jesus for *all* things, and a long, drawn-out discussion became the talk of the day. As we worked, I explained that according to the Word, "I can do all things through Christ, who strengthens me."

Joyce asked, "Does that mean *all* things?" I advised her that if the Word is true, and I believe it is, then that means *all* things.

Suddenly, without warning, Jesus had the opportunity to show His stuff. When we removed the fabric from the side over the legs, the wood brace fell to the floor, split in half. Obviously, the side was being held together by the extremely strong and well-placed fabric. After having paid a large price for the fabric and spent the time to cover the cushions, and all the other pieces were ready to be cut, the sofa was broken. I felt sick inside.

Now Joyce said, "Hey, just ask Jesus to fix it."

I knew in my heart she did not really believe that, and I suddenly was faced with if I really believed it, either. I could not be a stumbling block for my new baby-Christian sister, so I stopped and prayed. "Jesus, I need your help here. You know what is going on, and I pray that you will show your stuff just now."

We turned the sofa over, and decided to pull the two parts together, and I would get a nail and nail it through one side to the other. That meant I would have to angle the nail in just the right angle, or it would not work. I went to the garage to find a large nail, and there in front of me was a "10 penny" nail, as rusty as it could be. I continued to search, but no other was to be found.

So, in accordance with what I felt I had been led to do, I attempted to bang that nail into the very hard wood. We put it in on the bottom so as not to be seen or interfere with the upholstery. I banged, and banged, and banged some more. The nail was in almost halfway, and there it stopped; it would not budge any further. Not only that, but nor could I pull it out! Our situation was complicated even more.

We all know that Jesus was a carpenter, and He certainly would not have given me that nail and had me place it where I did for no good reason. But, now I was growing weary, and Joyce just looked at me questioningly.

I excused myself for a minute and went to the "throne of grace" in the bathroom and said, "Lord, you must have a mighty work going on here, and I am ready for it *now*."

About that time, Richard came in from work and immediately laughed at what I was trying to do. Certainly, this did not make things better, but all in good humor, I guess. He suggested that we needed a brace of some sort to screw into the bottom of the plate, and that would hold the two pieces together. I guess that is why God puts two people together, to make things work right!

Well, this certainly made sense to me, so we attempted the find a metal brace of some sort. We did indeed find a part of a brace for blinds, and it was strong enough to screw into the wood. But, first we had to be able to pull the two pieces together and hold them for the plate and screws to be put in. Then, there was that nail in the way. Richard tried with all his strength to pull the nail out to no avail. Joyce tried, and then again, I took the hammer. As I pulled the hammer, miraculously, the hammer head against the other piece forced it into perfect alignment. I just held the hammer with that nail until Richard screwed the plate into place. Perfect, strong, and we could cover it without it even being seen.

As we clapped and praised the Lord, I realized, *But, that nail!* We could not leave it hanging out like that. Richard suggested we bang it over and maybe it would not show. But, then Joyce said, halfway mocking again, "Ask Jesus to do it."

I insisted through His power all things can be done, so I went over to the nail and said, "In the name of Jesus, come out of there." We all laughed, but the laughing stopped, because with my thumb and forefinger and a gentle tug, that nail was in my hand. We all looked at each other in shock and total amazement. Jesus had indeed shown His power, and with such glory that we were all thankful. The sofa was upholstered and was used to give praise to God with every opportunity we had to share the story.

I was a rusty nail, as well, when Jesus chose me and made me a new person in Him. He is the maker of all things, indeed. "All things were made by him; and without him was not anything made that was made" (John 1:3). My sister received a precious gift from Jesus that day, as did I, and certainly Richard and the children benefited from it, as well. A small but powerful miracle to share, and one to encourage that indeed, "I can do all things through Christ who strengthens me."

Scot's Campfire

*"For whom the Lord loveth He correcteth; Even as a father
the son in whom he delighteth."*
—*Proverbs 3:12*

It was a real blessing to find out Richard and I were about to have a son born to us. Richard wanted an heir, but more so a son to be a companion. My little girl had been such a joy to me, to dress her up and show her off, Richard said, "Now is my turn. I want a son to play with." Well, now that blessing was about to happen: February 5, 1965, Richard got his wish.

Our son, Richard Scot, was born, finally. It seemed that he was never going to come: more than eleven months of carrying him, and even when the doctors figured it and said I was wrong, they had at this point to admit it had to be more than ten months. He weighed nine pounds, six ounces, and was twenty-three inches long—quite a large baby for a little woman like me.

I had had some severe problems delivering my daughter, so the doctors were really on edge about this time. My doctor had to be in Arizona . . . or Colorado . . . or somewhere West for a conference, and this made the upcoming event more scary. When my water broke, we knew this was the time. The doctors who were left in charge admitted me immediately to the hospital and prepared for all possible scenarios, lest the same occurrence should again raise its ugly head.

My primary doctor out in the West was called that I had been admitted. He was so concerned that he immediately caught the first plane back to attempt to be there for me. I, of course, did not know this, and was certainly a little spooked. Finally, when I was in the full swing of labor and had that wonderful trilene mask in hand, I was pretty relaxed. I looked up, and there he was! Dr. Meaders had made it back.

I remember I laughed and said, "You sorry rascal! What are you doing here?"

He just laughed and said, "I didn't want to miss the excitement." All went well, no problems, and our son came into this world looking half grown.

We thoroughly enjoyed our little girl and were in for quite a shock when this roustabout boy began to move around. He walked early and did everything early, and was really a handful from the beginning. He was in perpetual motion and into everything, and out of that, much more. He had dimples like his dad and a smile that would melt anyone's heart. So very personable that even when he was misbehaving, you could not help but smile at him. We found a very resourceful child who had a mind of his own. "Strong-willed" could not begin to describe this one.

I remember one day, while living in Florissant, Missouri, that I put him in his room for punishment. I put him on his bed and demanded he stay there. Later, I attempted to crack the door to see if he was asleep, and much to my horror, the door came off the hinges. He had found a screwdriver and loosened the screws! He was not on his bed, but had made himself a tent on the floor. Needless to say, I did not awaken him, but his dad awakened his bottom when he came home. This is just an inkling of what we faced with this child.

He was also the child who prayed, "God, I thank you for all my horses." We had no horses, but I knew someday we would with that prayer. He also would pray, "God, I thank you for good climbing trees, and please don't let any jolly green giants stomp our house down." He also cried out to me one day to come quick. I was alarmed at the excitement of his screeching, and ran to see what was wrong. He was standing at the front door and said, "Look! God just hung His Heaven out." He had discovered the sunset and the beauty overcame him. It just had to be Heaven. "All things are possible to him that believeth" (Mark 9:23).

Well, now to the miracle. It was a beautiful summer day, and Scot and two friends were playing in the backyard. It was quite safe in those days for children to play outside without constant monitoring—at least I thought so. This day, these little boys were romping in and out of the house and I was doing whatever inside. I heard them out by the carport, and I didn't go to see what was going on. I heard happy voices, not overly excited, and so I felt they were okay. WRONG!

As I continued to do my chores, I put a teapot on the gas stove and began to prepare dinner. The telephone rang. It was Richard, who always called on his way home to see if I needed anything. As I spoke to him, suddenly a strong wind blew and slammed the back door, literally blowing out the gas burners on the stove. Richard said, "What was that?"

I replied, "I don't know. It has been a balmy, quiet day with no breeze at all, and now there was a wind gust that slammed the door and blew out the stove!"

Richard replied, "God is at work about something, I guess."

I said goodbye and went to the stove to relight the burners. About that time, I heard the siren of fire trucks. They came down our street and went to the woods behind the house. I walked out onto the carport to see if I could see what was going on. Very soon, there came a fireman walking up through my yard, pulling Scot all along. The fireman asked, "Is this your child?"

I said, "Yes, what did he do?"

The fireman said, "You must be living right. I cannot see any possible way this boy was not burned to death." I sent Scot into the house, and the fireman explained that the boys had started a bonfire. It seemed Scot had seen his dad use gasoline to start a trash fire, and so Scot knew that the gasoline would make the fire "go faster and bigger." The fireman said, "I do not know how that gasoline did not splash back on him and burn him to death."

I could feel the hair raising on my head, and my whole body was trembling. I knew how he was not burned to death: God had sent a strange wind that blew the fire away from my child. A miracle, without a doubt, and certainly a great lesson. Children are always watching in even small things. We should always be aware of this at all times.

As I stated before, Richard adored his son, but now was the time to teach this boy a lesson, not to mention punish him. He certainly did not spare the rod, but also had to repent. Richard felt that his foolishness in using the gasoline was partly at fault. However, as the good dad he was, he talked to his son and reprimanded him, and apologized for being a poor example. He also took Scot to the fire station and made him apologize for wasting the firemen's time, and to thank them for coming and saving him. I believe that this impressed my boy.

I praise God again today as I write this account. My son, now a responsible, honest man, certainly knows this, and with precious grandchildren of his own, would remember and be what he knows God would have him to be and what he shows to them. To God be the Glory.

$\mathscr{D}$ear God, It's Cathy

"It is the Lord: let him do what seemeth him good."
—1 Samuel 3:18

I remember a terrifying miracle which we were never quite able to verify, but I know in my heart that it did indeed occur. This was shortly after we moved back from St. Louis, Missouri, and had renewed our friendship with our friends Bob and Sara. I had been concerned that Bob and Richard would renew their friendship and party and drink beer, and I was really against this relationship revival. As God would have it, though, my fears were unfounded, because Bob had become a born-again Christian, and eventually was the person who led my husband to receive Jesus as his savior.

Bob and Sara had given birth to a precious baby early in their marriage, but due to a RH factor, there were serious problems with the child. When less than a year old, the child had died, and our friends were devastated over her loss. They were very skeptical over the possibility of having another child and waited for a period of time. After Bob had received Christ, they felt that they wanted to try again, and now that they knew what the previous problem was, and they trusted Jesus for control of their lives, they chose to pursue this possibility. They were blessed with the birth of a baby daughter, Cathy, about a year following the birth of our son, Scot. Everyone was thrilled over this child, who was healthy and perfect in every way.

As couples, we spent a lot of time together, both in church and out of church. Bob and Richard were truly best friends. They were coleaders of the youth group at our church and shared many projects together.

Bob and Sara had a real blessing of a home given to them and were ready to move into this home. Of course, we were helping the move, loading up our station wagon and bringing many things from the previous residence to the new home. It was during this time that all the children were with me. Cathy and Scot were best little friends and wanted to be together, so I agreed to take them with me. We had pulled my Dodge Monaco into the backyard to unload, and then the children jumped into the backseat to go to my house. I started to pull forward to pull out of the yard, and suddenly I felt a terrible crunch. Fear grasped me like nothing I had ever known, especially when I stopped and looked back and saw the rear door open.

Scot screamed, "It's Cathy! She fell out!"

I froze with fear. I had felt the crunch, and knowing of nothing that had been in the yard to run over and not feeling this until the back wheels passed, I was terrified. I immediately jumped out of the car, but not before crying out to Jesus, "Please don't allow this, my fear, to happen, that I have run over our precious Cathy."

As I rounded the car, Cathy came running, looking at me with startling fear, and crying. I took her in to her mother, and through all the hysteria I attempted to relay the happening. We took Cathy into the bedroom and checked her completely. There were no bruises, marks, or anything that would indicate she had been run over. We asked her what happened, but she was too young to relate exactly what did happen.

We went out in the yard to see what could have made the sound and crunching feeling of the tire, but there was nothing to indicate anything of the sort. To this day, we are not sure of what happened that day, but in my heart, I will always believe that I did indeed run over Cathy, but God protected her from all harm. Could this have been a warning, and not an actuality? Who knows? I certainly knew from that time forward to be very sure rear doors were locked and children were appropriately protected.

God has a way of teaching us with real possibilities to perhaps ward off any future tragedy. I believe to this day, and can still feel the crunch of the rear tire. I believe Bob and Sara were awarded a miracle that day for their obedience and service. I praise God for the blessing of remembering that He is able to do all things, even restore a child who had been smashed by a car tire.

Bob and Sara lived in the house less than a year. They accepted the call of God to serve with Campus Crusades for Christ, where they served until Bob's death and Sara's retirement. Cathy is a grown, wonderful, Christian mother. I praise God for this memory and miracle.

$\mathcal{K}$a-plunk!

"For your father in heaven knows the things you have need of before you ask."
—Matthew 6:8

I t was 1968, and we had just moved back to Georgia from the St. Louis area. Our home had been rented out during the time we were in Missouri, and so we were very happy to once again be in our home. Unfortunately, the renters had not taken care of it, as I would have, and a lot of things had to be done to bring it back to what I wanted it to be.

Richard had suffered some illness while there in Missouri, and we decided it would be in our best interest to come back where I had family. We knew that his illness was one that was progressive and came in intervals. I had a work record here, and felt that if necessary, I could find a job with some of my old employers. Also, we had good church friends and family. Ultimately, the decision was made to move back to Georgia.

As we prepared for our move, I remembered how Richard and our friend Bob would drink beer and become a little drunk. So, on the moving day, when the movers were loading up, I stopped and prayed, "Lord, please don't take us this far to only have Richard be back with Bob and the excessive drinking start again."

As we arrived at our home in Georgia, we had hardly unloaded the furniture when the doorbell rang, and you guessed it: there was Bob and Sara. I hugged Sara, said hello to Bob, and walked into the living room. Sara and I were chatting, and Bob and Richard walked outside.

Soon they came in, both in tears. Richard came over and hugged me, while Bob spoke, "Roni, I want you to meet my new friend, Richard." I looked at Bob, questioning, when he said, "Well, new person." Richard had just prayed with Bob and received Jesus as his Lord. This changed our lives completely.

Richard had worked as a supervisor with Chrysler Corporation in Fenton, Missouri, and had a good work record. However, his illness had taken a toll on our finances. Now back in Marietta, a new job search began. Fortunately, he was able to secure employment with the Chrysler Parts Depot in Southeast Atlanta. Though it was quite a distance to drive each day, the pay was good and certainly better than any jobs near where we lived.

Richard had to drive to and from, and spent a great deal of time on the road. Before leaving Missouri, he had purchased a new Plymouth Satellite hardtop convertible, dark green and with all the bells and whistles. He was really proud of his car. Every time he walked past it, he would shine any smudge with his shirt sleeve, and to be sure, kept it washed and waxed regularly. The kids knew not to get near Daddy's new car. They certainly did not eat or drink in that car. It was well cared for.

We had become a member of a sharing group where we gathered with other friends at the home of one of the members. One of the main things that was being taught was, "In all things to give thanks, that God could use the bad for our good and for His glory." Well, this would soon try our belief and faith in such. Certainly, we were in a new groove, since Richard had now become a Christian and was growing leaps and bounds. The pride of the car was about to get in the way, though.

On this Friday morning, Richard headed out to work as usual. All things were well—until the drive home. It was raining very heavily, and the traffic was a real horror. As Richard was coming down the expressway, the car in front of him suddenly slammed on its brakes, and with the slick road and not too much time, Richard tried to stop. Unfortunately, the slick was too much, and he skidded into the car in front.

He was sick to his stomach about his new car being wrecked. The police came and determined that it was no fault of his nor anyone else, so all were to take care of their own damages. I was waiting for his call, as he always did when he got to the Cobb County line, but he had not called. I looked at the clock and knew it was past time, so I began to be concerned that something was wrong.

Finally, the call came, and Richard told me that he had been involved in an accident. He was at a pay phone at a nearby service station. I asked him, "Did you thank God for the wreck?"

He quickly answered with a laugh, "You know I did, I really did."

I answered, "Then all will be okay. Hurry on home."

Well, he came home with a badly twisted bumper, broken headlight, and a crinkled fender. Really sad over the damage to his car, he called his insurance broker. He lived right around the corner from our house and said he would come by on Saturday morning and look at the mess. Sure enough, on Saturday morning he came over, looked at the car, and told Richard to get three estimates and bring them to him.

Richard set out to do just that, all before noon on Saturday, because they closed at noon on Saturdays. The average estimate was approximately $375. So, Richard was trying to decide when he could give his car up for a day to have it repaired. Come Monday morning, he drove to work, and oddly enough, where he usually parked, the lot was full and he had to go to the other side, parking near the dumpster where old parts were put to be carried to salvage. You guessed it: right there on the top of the dumpster was a chrome bumper in perfect condition, the very bumper that fit his car.

Excited, he went to his supervisor and asked if he might be allowed to purchase that bumper. He was told that the dumpster had already been weighed and that bumper was part of the estimated cost, but a twisted one would weigh the same, so go ahead, but hurry before they came to pick up the dumpster. Richard always had a toolbox in his car, so he went to work immediately, and in no time at all he had the old, twisted bumper removed and the new one installed, and none too soon, as the truck was now there to haul the dumpster off.

His car didn't look too bad at all. So, on his way home he stopped at a store called Thrift City and purchased the appropriate headlight for only $3.78. When he arrived at home, he was met by the kids, and I went out to greet him. He was removing the old, broken headlight and now had the new one in place. He bragged about how great the car looked with the new bumper and headlight, and exclaimed, "If it were not for this crinkled fender . . ."

With that statement, he took his fist and hit the fender just about where the worst of the crinkle was. Suddenly, the fender said, "Ka-plunk!" and out popped the dents completely. The children and I stood there in shock and disbelief, as did Richard. No scratch, no dent, no pick hole, nothing! It looked just as it did new. Richard laughed and pointed to the sky, like you know this came from God.

Well, almost immediately, Richard called the adjuster, who came by the next afternoon and issued us a check for $375. This check gave us enough money to buy groceries and gas for Richard to get us through until a payday some three weeks later.

Thanking God when it is not really something to be thankful for certainly was a good thing for us, then. We shared the story many times, and it was a wonderful testimony for our children to tell, as well. God had come through for us in a way we would never have chosen, but did not hurt us or even inconvenience us, but rather supplied our needs from His riches in glory.

God can make a way when there is no way, and we remember this miracle as evidence. He was faithful to us, and we give Him the praise, more so for Richard's salvation, which carried him through until his death. No other gift or anything can compare to eternal life with Him.

That day, Richard was given that assurance.

$\mathscr{S}$mall Miracles of Joy

"And we know that all things work together for good to them that love God, to them who are the called according to his purpose."
—Romans 8:28

What does it take to have a real miracle? Well, as far as I am concerned, it is something that is totally unlikely and without understanding as to how it happened otherwise. So, having said this, I will share a couple of small miracles that I enjoyed some years back.

The first one was regarding my "addiction" to the telephone. It seemed that I spent a great deal of my day just talking to whomever would like to talk to me on the phone. Sometimes this would translate into most of the day! Housework was done with the phone on my shoulder with a long cord. In those days, there were no remote phones, so long cords were necessary to walk around and talk. I did most everything while carrying on a conversation with a "friend."

This was one of those days. I had lots of housework to do and clothes to wash, etc., and talking on the phone would take precedence over these things.

Enter my dear friend Sara. Sara was one that I talked to every day, and when the phone rang and it was her, I was pleased. Sara had called me, though, to invite me to a ladies' Bible study in the area. I had heard of these gatherings and was certainly interested, but today I felt a bit draggy and did not wish to dress and go. When Sara insisted that I come with her, she overcame my objections. She stated the kids are in school, you really don't have anything else more important, and most of all, you will just talk on the phone.

I was stuck. I knew she was right, but I insisted, "I believe God wants me to clean my house today."

Immediately, she laughed and shamed me for such, and said, "Now, you and I know full well, you will not clean your house, but will talk on the phone all day." I knew she knew me well, and she certainly had my number. I protested and insisted that I would indeed do my work. Sara warned, "God heard you say this, so you better clean your house." Well, I agreed, and that was the end of the phone call.

I hung the phone up and untangled the cord, and began to walk down the hallway to my bedroom. You guessed it: the phone started to ring. Quickly, I began to apologize to God and alibi that I did not do the calling, that that was someone calling me. I walked to the phone and said, "Hello?"

The voice on the other end of the line said, "Ma'am, this is the repairman for Southern Bell, and we are going to be working on the phone lines in your area today. Your phone will be out of service until four o'clock p.m."

For the first time in my life, I realized that my God had a sense of humor. I could see Him smiling, as if to say "Gotcha!" Needless to say, I cleaned my house, and never again did I blame God for my refusal to go a Bible study.

Several days later, I had another encounter with God regarding the telephone. Another account about this: I had been to a Bible study on another day, and the topic was "ask and you shall receive." The leader further stated that sometimes, no was an answer, and that sometimes, the answer could interfere with another person's will, so to consider that when we ask of God.

Today, I was busy in the house when I realized I had not seen my daughter for a while. She was then seven years old, and we were in a safe neighborhood, but I kept an eye on her. I looked outside and called to her, and she was nowhere in sight. The Bible-study leader had said that there were times when we needed for God to answer our prayer immediately, and He certainly would do so if it did not violate any of His principles.

I continued to call, and walked to the end of the street to look and increased the volume of my voice. Still, no Kelli. I was beginning to get nervous. Where was she, and why was she not answering me? I knew that I had put her into God's worthy hands, but, nevertheless, I was concerned.

After calling several neighbors and not getting any answers, I did what the Bible-study teacher suggested: I went back to the house and stood on the porch, and I called out to my God, "Lord, I need to know where she is, and I want to know right now!" I stood and looked and waited, stating, "Lord, I am waiting."

The telephone began to ring, and I was certainly not going to answer that phone. I was waiting for the Lord to bring Kelli around the corner of one of the houses. As I waited breathlessly, I watched and the phone rang. Again, I said, "I am waiting, Lord." The phone would not stop ringing, so I ran to the phone with the extra-long cord and pulled it to the porch, where I had been standing, and said, "Hello?"

The voice on the phone said to me, "Mama, were you looking for me?" It was my daughter, and she was checking in.

Again, I saw God smile. You see, I asked Him to find her, and then I was telling Him how to let me know. So, He was telling me, "It isn't the phone that is at fault, but your priorities." I certainly understood that and tried to do better.

Both of these little miracles were teaching prods for me, and I have never forgotten them. Do I still try to orchestrate what I want done? Sure, but I certainly know that just because He does not do it as I think it should be done, won't stop Him for taking care of the matter. I praise God for all the small miracles He has performed in my life.

The Christmas Card

"I am come that they might have life, and that they may have it more abundantly."
—John 10:10

There was a difficult time when we were awaiting disability that food was of very short supply and also money was nonexistent. It was now approaching the Christmas season. Our daughter Jenna was still very young and believed in Santa Claus. She had begun to give us her list for Santa to fill. I could not bring myself to tell such a little child that her dreams were unable to be filled. So, with other, more serious things having been answered, once again I went to my God and asked Him to be in charge.

As the days passed, it seemed that there was no help in sight. I started going to yard sales to see if I could find some of the things she had on her list. I remember one sale in particular, Jenna was with me, and there was a Madame Alexander baby doll there. It had its eyelashes pulled out, and the hair was almost gone, and it was dirty, but Jenna fell in love with that doll. I told her that if she got that doll, then she could not expect Santa to bring her another. She agreed; she really wanted that doll. It cost very little, so we brought it home. It was just the size of a newborn, so I was also able to find some clothes for it at another sale. At least she had something she wanted. I decided I would get the clothes ready without her knowledge, and was able to get some false eyelashes to repair the eyes, and worked on the rooted hair until it looked pretty good.

I told no one about our lack of funds, but continued to look for secondhand things that looked new that I could afford to buy. Then, a miracle occurred. As I arrived home from work one day, my neighbor came across the street with an envelope. She said that a lady had brought it to her door. She said that she had seen a silver Buick in my driveway, but did not see who it was. The car had stopped in front of her house just as she was going in out of her yard. She had been out there, as she was every morning, watering her plants. She said that the lady came to her door and asked if she knew me. My neighbor told her she knew me well. The lady asked if she would be so kind as to give me a card for her, and my neighbor agreed to do so.

Paulette laughed and said, "Now, if that was the millionaire, I get some of it." You may recall that there had been a TV show in which a millionaire chose a special person each week to give a million dollars to. We laughed, and I walked into the house.

Just then, as I was returning home, Jenna came running to me to welcome me home, and then Richard was there to tell about the day. I laid the card down on the commode there in the foyer and forgot about it until much later that night. After I had put Jenna to bed, I walked to lock the front door, prepare to do the dishes, and get myself ready for bed. It was then that I noticed the card and picked it up to open it. Richard walked up and asked what it was, and I related the sequence of events to him. With that, I opened the card: there inside was a crisp $100 bill with a note that said, "This is for Jenna's Christmas," signed Santa. I was amazed and thrilled, but who could have done this? I knew that whoever did had just been responding to my Lord, because He was the only one who knew I needed it.

I later shared with my neighbor about it, and inquired as to what the lady looked like. The description did not match anyone I knew, nor did the vehicle she was div-ing. To this day, I do not know who the lady was, but I knew who sent her and praised Him for it.

Christmas came and went, with everything Jenna wanted there for her to enjoy. Richard and I felt we had received a miracle/blessing, indeed: a special gift from the Father. Perhaps there is someone in need that you have knowledge of. Be obedient to our Lord when He calls you to help. The blessing will certainly be shared by the other person, but especially by you.

Scot's Fishing Trip

"That if you confess with your mouth the Lord Jesus and believe in your heart that God has raised Him from the dead, you will be saved."
—*Romans 10:9*

When the father in the home becomes ill, all the family is affected. The children become somewhat insecure. I found that it affected my son more than my daughters. My son always had a wonderful relationship with his dad, and Richard was always there to teach him the things about which a man should know. He helped his dad work on cars, air conditioners, plumbing, yard work, etc. Also, they enjoyed fishing, Indian guides, and camping. So, when my husband became more and more disabled, it affected Scot a great deal. Especially, he felt this way when Dad could no longer share his fun times and go with him.

Our up-the-street neighbor owned a plumbing company, and his sons worked with him. They were Scot's age and very close friends. Mr. Roach loved being with his boys, and he felt compassion for Scot's loss. Because of this, Mr. Roach decided to hire Scot to work for him, as well, doing helper jobs of clean-up, gofer-type things. This gave Scot a little bit of money, and more important, a feeling of worth.

Every year, Mr. Roach took all his employees on a deep-sea fishing trip as a reward for their faithful work. Now Scot, who was only fourteen years old at the time, had his first chance to go on the trip. He had saved all the money he had earned and had enough to pay his way.

Mom was not so sure about this. The ocean? Grown men who may be having beer, etc.? Well, I was a little unnerved, and would certainly like to have a good reason for him not to go. The doctors for whom I worked really shamed me for feeling this way, but I was an overprotective mom, and I really did not want to trust anyone else with my son.

As time drew near, I became more fearful. Finally, I decided to ask God—listen to this—to find a way for him to legitimately not be able to go. You know that God does not interfere with someone's will. I did not dare to ask in His will, though. I just did not want Scot to go.

Three days before the trip, I got my wish. Scot misbehaved, and now I had the opportunity to cancel his fishing trip. He was crushed, though he knew he had misbehaved and deserved the punishment. Mom was indeed relieved.

But, guess what? Dad confronted me and said, "Roni, that kid has worked and saved for a whole year for this trip. I know he did wrong, but I think the punishment is a bit harsh, in view of how hard he has worked for it."

Well, overprotective me began having feelings of guilt. Just looking at my son and how sad he was really broke my heart. Then, the boys, with their sad faces and begging, didn't help, either. I prayed about it and again talked to my husband, who suggested I put a stiff work order on Scot: have him cut the entire yard (Scot hated yard work), weed eat, and blow and groom the area. That was a tall job for him, but I thought it reasonable. So, I called Scot in and told him of my decision. He accepted joyfully to do this work.

I went about my business cleaning and vacuuming, when suddenly I heard quite a ruckus outside. There, on my front lawn, were three riding mowers and two weed whackers all going at the same time. All his friends had come over to help with his "punishment." This was not the deal, and I was not happy.

I allowed the boys to finish all the work, and they came in for my approval. They had done an exceptional job, but did not expect what happened then. I told them that Scot had not done the work as agreed, but had allowed others to take his punishment, and now he still stood guilty of the infraction, as he had not paid the price to forgive his fault. Once again, the boys and Scot looked downhearted and began to beg.

I looked at my husband and said, "What now?"

He said, "Ask God." God always has a plan, so I did as my husband suggested and consulted Him.

Knowing that the boys did not go to church, though Scot was deprived of his father due to illness, these boys were deprived of the Heavenly Father. I was certain that they had probably never picked up a Bible, so I submitted the following: "Boys, there is a scripture in the Bible that states that if you do *this*, thou shalt be saved. Find me that scripture and have Scot memorize it to quote word for word, and I will consider his debt paid in full."

They were excited, and each was given a Bible to begin their search. Then Scot asked, "Can I ask someone to get the answer?"

I said, "Sure, ask anyone you want."

Immediately, he called my neighbor down the street. He knew Pat was a dedicated Christian, and surely she would know how easy would that be. Well, Pat acknowledged that she knew the scripture to quote, but could not off the top of her head remember where to find it. Then he called his Aunt Joy, Aunt Harriet, and others to no avail. So, the boys began to read and search.

As time was passing rapidly, and they were to leave at 2:00 p.m., they felt overwhelmed, to say the least. Then, Tony, whom we thought was not the brightest penny in the drawer, showed his common sense, and said, "Mrs. Z., we ain't ever going to find that in time! There are too many words in this book."

With that, his older brother chimed in with, "Can't you give us a hint?"

Now they had asked everyone they could think of, and now they had been reading the Bible for some thirty minutes to no avail. I said, "Okay, it is in the book of Romans."

They said, "Let's find Romans."

Again, Tony spoke up and said, "Look in the front and it tells you what page it is on."

Now, we were moving. Alan said, "Tony, you take number one. Bobby, you take two, Scot, three, and I will take four."

They continued to read. After four chapters, still nothing that said "thou shalt be saved." Now, on to the next four chapters. Still, no one found the scripture.

Tony again spoke up. "Mrs. Z, are you sure it is in this book?"

I replied, "Yes, I am very sure."

Now Alan said, "I will take nine. Tony, you take ten, Bobby, eleven, and Scot, twelve."

I got more and more excited as I watched them searching the scriptures, knowing full well that some of this Word had to sink into their spirits.

Suddenly, Tony shouted, "I got it! I got it! It is in the tenth chapter and in the number-nine line."

They all turned to Romans 10:9 and read it out loud together. They were jumping and shouting. As I am typing this, I am laughing to tears in remembrance. They said, "Zub, you can go, man! You can go!"

Well, it was 1:00 p.m. now. They had read through their lunchtime and felt safe at this point. Then, I said, "Hey, wait a minute. There is another part of this, you know. Scot has to be able to quote it from memory."

You can guess what happened next. They were all coaching Scot to be able to quote the scripture. Hearing them correcting him and repeating the scripture over and over to him was sheer joy in my spirit. Finally, Scot came down from his room and they all stood there while he performed. Not only did Scot perform, but all four boys had memorized this most valuable scripture.

All was well, and Scot had his duffel bag ready to leave. It was then that his dad called him over and opened his personal Bible, which one of the boys was using. There, in the front cover, was written, "How to be saved, Romans 10:9-10." As he showed this to his son, Scot and the boys looked at Richard, and Scot asked, "Dad, you knew it all the time. Why didn't you tell me?"

Then, the best one-liner ever was spoken to my son and a life lesson for us all: "Son, you didn't ask me."

As I am typing this, again I am convicted. How often do I ask everyone I know before I finally ask the only one who can do anything about it? How often do we not consult our Father? Truly, God had a purpose for this and a lesson for us all. He makes this very clear in His Word: James 4:2, "Ye have not, because ye ask not." He is faithful to his word, and in Matthew 7:7 reminds us to "ask and it shall be given you."

Just four years ago, Alan came to install some plumbing in my new home. I reminded him about this, and tears came to his eyes as he said, "I remember that, Mrs. Z," and he related the story to his helper. This was indeed a miracle that God brought to four young men. His Word never is void, but at the time needed, the Holy Spirit will bring it back to remembrance. I feel that God directed this occasion to bless some kids who may have never received the Word needed for their salvation. It could take a lifetime for them, but indeed, God will keep it in their spirit until He chooses to bring it forth. To God be the Glory in all that was accomplished that day.

You would think after such a miraculous day and the blessings received, I would be at peace. Well, I am a flawed Christian, and fear still gripped me about the trip. When the boys had not called by 10:00 p.m., I was very scared. I called Mrs. Roach, and she stated that she had not heard a word. The other mothers were concerned, as well, but I should have known that I could trust my God.

I finally went to bed and tossed and turned, and prayed that God would dispatch an angel to watch over my boy. Approximately midnight, I was awakened and had a strange feeling of a presence in the room. As I looked through the dark, there stood a strong young man, approximately in his thirties, with a handkerchief folded into a sweatband around his head and wearing swim trunks. He spoke not a word audibly, but his spirit spoke to mine and said, "Fear not, for I am watching over your son." With that, he disappeared, and I had such peace that I immediately fell asleep and awakened in the morning refreshed with no fear whatsoever.

Mrs. Roach called and said, "The kids were hungry, so Mr. Roach had taken them directly to eat at a popular fish restaurant there in Panama City, and then to a game mall. They had not gotten back to the motel until late, so that is why there was no call."

All was well. The boys were happy and safe, and now on the ship out to sea to catch a big fish. When my son returned, I questioned him as to whether or not he saw the person I described that came to me, but he did not remember seeing anyone of that description. Whether there physically or in spirit, I am sure that my God did indeed dispatch an angel to watch over my son.

I learned a great lesson that day and night, and certainly I never questioned whether or not my God was in full control of all situations, and I trust Him more and more. It sometimes takes me a real shaking by my Father to get my attention, but mostly He always is gentle and chastens me with such love, I almost treasure the shaking.

The scriptures say to spare the rod and spoil the child, and I agree with that, but this occasion was not only a reprimand, punishment, or whatever you would call it, but it was a blessing and a better way because it was God's way. Jesus said, "Suffer little children . . . to come unto me: for of such is the kingdom of heaven" (Matthew 19:14). I believe that this is true, and lest we come to him as a little child, we may not be received at all.

I pray that you are blessed by this story and will choose to try a like reprimand instead of a physical rebuke. A little love and understanding go a long way, especially if directed by our Father.

*J*ay Jay, the Boy Who Wouldn't

"The Lord that delivered me out of the paw of the lion . . . He will deliver me out of the hand of this Philistine."
—1 Samuel 17:37

This is the story of the boy who wouldn't submit to the world—a boy who was not supposed to be able to do anything—and the way God moved in a miraculous way to bring this boy to manhood in a most glorious way.

"Jay Jay" stood for "Joyce and Jerry." This was their child, and since birth, he was always known as Jay Jay. This was my sister's fifth child, and one which would bless us all with his humble spirit and Godly nature. Jay was born with minimal brain dysfunction, ADHD, and dyslexia. He was slow in his milestones, and just seemed not to be able to function as other children.

At the time of a checkup when a young baby, the doctor called my sister and brother-in-law in and said he had the test results on Jay. They were not encouraging at all. As a matter of fact, it was a near horror story. My sister and her husband were told that this child would always be a child, with little or no abilities. He had brain dysfunction that was, though said to be minimal, actually very debilitating, and would keep him from functioning as a normal child and certainly not to be a normal adult. It was advised that they begin right now to provide for him, because, as the doctor said, "He will never be able to provide for himself, never be a normal man," but would have to be taken care of always.

With this horrifying news, my sister's husband went into real mourning. He could not accept that his son, who bore his name, would be handicapped. He was a proud man and looked forward to the birth of this son, and now he was being told that he was never to mature, never one he could be proud of. This was a shock beyond anything he had even considered. He began to pull away from the boy and put a wall between them. He just could not accept this, and his denial was debilitating.

On the other hand, my sister, being a woman of God, would not accept this, but constantly prayed over her son. She attempted to present him in as much normality as possible, believing that God could change anything if it was His will, and why would he not use this child as a miracle for Him?

He was a happy child, but in perpetual motion, into and out of everything. It was suggested that he be medicated with a medication that had been used for this disorder for some time, but my sister did not believe in this "stuff." She read everything she could find and began a real regime of no sugar, no preservatives, no wheat, no dairy, and anything else she could read that could be in any way detrimental.

Jay, though a "wild child," was an obedient child, and was willing to forgo candy and all the good stuff other kids had. He also was trying to be so obedient to his dad that perhaps he could win his love. Jay was indeed unusual and really precious, certainly a God-filled youngster. My sister kept him in the Word, filled with God's promises and hope always. Jay was saturated with the Word of God to the extent that he wanted to live that Word and do so as much as his little heart could understand.

When five years old, he was taken to preschool. Now, the problems would begin. Before this, his dyslexia was not known. He was really having trouble. He saw things backward. No one knew this; they only knew he was not excelling in his studies. It was assumed that he was immature and should be kept out of school another year. He was known to wander about over the room, and was distracting to the other children. Testing was ordered, which would confirm the ADHD. They would try to force the medication on him, or else he would be removed from the school.

As I stated before, my sister disagreed with this and decided she would attempt to homeschool him rather than have him medicated. All possible herbs and diet had been taken into consideration. Jay was just not improving. In despair, his dad was insisting he have something to counteract this, and try to give him something of a normal life. My sister still believed God and tried not to do this. Out of submission to her husband, they would finally try this, at least for a time. There was a new drug on the market that had been reported not to have so many side effects and was recommended for the exact condition from which Jay suffered.

Out of sheer frustration, the medication was begun.

Jay was now so docile, he was never happy as before, only slow, and always looked as though he was in deep thought, but somewhere else. As the dosage was put up and down, and off and on, there was a real dilemma if this was the right thing for him at all. He had not done much better in school, and came home crying most of the time because the kids and teacher were laughing at him. When questioned closely, Jay related how he knew the answer to the question, but when asked to write it on the board, they all laughed. He could see what it said, but to the others and teacher, it was gibberish and undefinable.

Suddenly, while he was describing this, his mom felt a word from the Lord and asked him to write what he had written for the teacher. Immediately after writing, my sister took it to the bathroom mirror. Wow, what a shocker! Jay was writing all the answers correctly, only backward. Jay was dyslexic.

Something could be done to help him. My sister went to the school counselor and showed her what she had discovered. Why, in all the testing, did they not uncover this? Why didn't they take the time to see what was going on with him? After all, my sister and her husband were paying a large tuition for him to attend this private school, and his needs were not being addressed at all. As a matter of fact, her son was being ridiculed by the teachers, as well as the students. Certainly, they deserved more than this. Angry and disappointed, they demanded a refund of tuition, and after a threat of suit, it was done.

The search began for another school. This time, a Christian school was found and checked out completely. Jay began to attend, although he was two years behind the grade he was supposed to be in. Jay did well here, and the people worked with him. My sister made friends with another mother who had nearly the same experiences as her own. Together, the two women went on a crusade to help their embattled children, and through much prayer and fasting, they, as two, were able to be strong enough to make things happen.

The boys became best friends, because they understood each other, and now that they had a friend, they were happy and glad to work on their studies. This friendship continued until the boys were almost in high school.

They wanted to be off the medication. There was a warning about the withdrawal of this medication. There were some reports of severe depression, and suicide had been noted, making caution paramount. Research brought information regarding a doctor in Washington, DC, who had a great deal of success in detoxification of this medication. The two women made appointments, and off they went with their boys to be evaluated.

The treatment was a long span of special foods and nutrients, and gradual reduction of the medication. Urine tests were done daily to get the content of the medication in the system with any other altering chemicals that the medication had produced. It looked promising, and they elected to try this.

Before going home, the boys wanted to go to the Smithsonian Institute and see the dinosaurs. So, they hailed a tour bus and went on the tour of Washington, including the museum. They were told at what time to meet the tour bus back out front, and when that time came, my sister asked Jay to step outside to see if the bus was there. Jay was now eighteen years old and over six feet tall, slender, and quite a handsome young man. He had a soft, reddish hair, large hazel eyes, and dimples, and was indeed a handsome guy. As big and strong as he was, my sister was not at all concerned for him to go outside to check on the bus. She would soon find out Washington was not like their hometown.

Jay did not come back immediately, and she felt a tug in her spirit. So, she went out to check, just in time to see Jay being dragged down the street by two guys toward a waiting van. She screamed to let him go, and then cried, "Jesus, help him!" With that, the men dropped him and jumped into the van and sped off. Jay was all right but very shaken up, and so was my sister. Jesus had come through miraculously in a very scary situation. Jay was not surprised, because this was not the first time Jesus had come through for him.

He remembered to the other woman and her son when he had had meningitis. He had a very high fever and was suffering with his head with such intense pain, he could hardly stand it. When he was admitted to the emergency room, he was immediately diagnosed with meningitis, but a spinal tap had to confirm. There was a Jewish doctor on call there, and he was attempting to comfort Jay regarding the spinal tap. Jay, just nine years old, turned to his mother and said, "Pray, Mama, pray."

Pray, she did. The Jewish doctor stood quietly while my sister laid hands on Jay and prayed. The doctor walked out of the room to get the spinal tray for the puncture. When he returned, what a shock he had to find that Jay was out of pain, no fever, and sitting up asking for something to drink. Jay was instantly healed, and walked out of the emergency room to the total amazement and unbelief of the doctor in charge. The powerful name of Jesus brought a miracle to Jay that day.

Jay was now old enough to consider getting a job. He did not have any skills, but was interested in getting some kind of a job. His dad was quite concerned that he was not going to be self-supporting, so they set up a trust fund for him, just in case. My sister had no doubt that Jesus was with Jay in all things, and though he would have to be tested, he would be victorious. She believed this, and told Jesus every day how much she loved Him for what He was doing in Jay's life.

Jobs were not good to Jay. People really don't act very well to God's people, and

Jay showed his Christian belief and walked the walk. Many were blessed by him, but others were cruel. I remember once he was working for a popular grocery chain as a stock boy. He worked during the busy hours, and the ones with whom he was working were quite the rough types. As they talked about sex and porn, Jay would walk away. It was not in his vocabulary to use the kind of words they used, and Jay was committed to Jesus and did not participate in these things. One day when they had been teasing him, he told them that he had taken an oath to Jesus to remain pure until marriage. This really incensed these guys. So, they went to the microphone, which was heard all over the store, and announced, "Jay is a virgin." This was humiliating for this to be announced. He was proud that he was true to what Christ wanted for him, but he did not want this to be advertised.

Later that evening, some of the boys grabbed him, held him in a sexual display, and made fun of him. He attempted to report this to the manager, and was told, "If you can't stand the heat, get out of the kitchen."

Jay left that job that night. He proclaimed, "I will not do anything to humiliate my Jesus, nor will I associate with those who do." Jay refused to submit to the things of the world. God would reward him for being faithful.

After many attempts in the workforce, Jay came to his mom and told her he felt that he was called into the ministry. After much prayer, it was decided that Jay would begin classes at a church in another city. Jay drove the 150-mile trip daily and studied very diligently. We all laughed because we felt that his mom deserved a degree, as well, because she, too, studied with him in all things. Jay did well, and finally received his associate's degree in theology. He would begin to use what he had learned.

Shortly thereafter, he had the opportunity to go on a mission trip. We were all thrilled for him, but Jay had never been anywhere without his mom, and concern as to whether or not he could handle this was great. The pastor of his church assured that the mission team was well represented with responsible people, and that Jay would be taken care of. So began Jay's calling and subsequent ministry. After this mission, there was one to Mexico, then Peru, and then to Romania and Africa. Jay was on his way to what he felt God had called him to do.

It was now time to put a life's work into place so that Jay would have a livelihood. So, once again, Mom and Dad decided to jump into the works. Jay had been scheduled to go to Romania for a second trip, which he did not want to attend, but was obedient to the Lord. It just so happened that this time there were no responsible adults to accompany him. As a matter of fact, the others on the team had never before been on a mission trip. As my sister, his mom, prayed for his protection, suddenly Jay stepped up and was the adult on this mission. He just took charge, as if he were the old pro in it all, and became just that. God supplied all that he needed to do what had to be done. Also, an extra blessing, because during this trip he met the young woman who he would eventually make his wife and partner in his mission.

His mom and dad helped him to purchase a residence and renovate it for a school and living quarters, and then his mission was set up. Jay moved to Romania, where he lives with his wife and two children.

Jay was indeed delivered from the paw of the lion and all the Philistines of his life. And yes, he and his dad became close friends. Certainly Jerry, his dad, has the highest respect for his son and is so very proud of what God has done.

Jay lost his beloved mother in the winter of 2007. This loss was devastating to him, but he pretty much runs his mission alone. Support is very shallow at this point, but with all that the Lord has done in Jay's life, no one questions but that Jay will continue to do well through the one he trusts most of all: Jesus.

Jay Jay, the boy who wouldn't go with the world, stands as a true man of God, a true blessing to all who come in contact with him. What a miracle! What a wonderful work credited only to the Almighty King of Kings and Lord of Lords. There is nothing too hard for our Lord, and this was shown through the grace He displayed with Jay Jay.

An Issue of Blood

"And a woman having an issue of blood twelve years, which had spent all her living upon physicians, neither could be healed of any, Came behind Him, and touched the border of His garment: and immediately her issue of blood stanched."
—*Luke 8:43–44*

My sister, Joyce, and I were almost as close as twins. We were born twenty-one months apart, and all of our lives we were just the closest. It seemed that we were really bound together not only by blood, but by belief and likes, as well. At some time, it proved a problem in our teen years, because we seemed to like the same boys for boyfriends, as well. Always, we thought more of each other than the boys, and therefore, we never fought over such. I had a real big crush on the man she eventually married, but it seemed that his heart just went to her, so I stepped aside.

Over the years, I lived with them at intervals, and always and in all ways, Joe was my big brother. He looked after me, but never allowed me to know that if it were not Joyce, then it certainly would have been me. We truly loved each other and trusted each other completely.

As with all things, there are sometimes when mistakes are made and consequences have to be paid. Thus was the case in Joyce and Joe's marriage, which resulted in impending divorce. It was during a time when their differences were being resolved when Joyce learned she was pregnant. This was a very dangerous thing for her. She had developed a problem with blood clots and had been placed on the medication Coumadin, which would thin the blood. This was not something that could be tolerated in pregnancy. She either had to stop the medication and chance blood clots, which could kill her, or abort her baby.

Joyce was a Christian and could not see "killing" her baby. There were many days of great stress, and her physicians had made the determination that she would have to abort the fetus within the next three days. Joyce called me in tears and cried to me, "Sis, please pray that God will forgive me. I have no choice, according to the doctors."

Also, the surgery to remove the fetus was dangerous, as well. I did indeed begin to pray, and asked God to allow me to help my sister.

On the third day, when she was scheduled to go in for the abortion, she awakened with an issue of blood—not extensive, but sufficient to spontaneously abort the fetus. God had answered her prayers. He terminated the pregnancy, but she had no hemorrhaging at all. It was complete and clean, and there were no complications.

If this was all there was to this story, it would be pretty much general, but though it was not time for my menses to occur, at the exact time my sister was aborting the fetus, I began to hemorrhage. I was not aware of it until I stood up at work and the blood gushed, soaking my entire lower half. It required me to put a towel around me and go to the car and home. By the time I reached home, the car was also soaked. I got off my feet, and within several hours the blood stopped completely and there was no problem for me at all.

God took care of the problem with Joyce and allowed me to suffer the hemorrhage that my sister could not tolerate. This may sound strange, but I know that this was true. I had been a stand-in for my sister and her issue of blood, and the Lord had healed us both. Joyce and I have shared this miracle with many other people who confirmed similar things happening to them with a close sibling. We praise God for being our Daddy in the absence of our daddy. Praise and honor to our God.

You are probably wondering if the marriage survived this loss of a child. Well, no, the marriage was not reunited. The pregnancy possibly would have held the marriage together, but there was another miracle on the way. God had a new plan, and this one would bring forth many miracles through another child that God chose to use for His service. A son referred to as Jay Jay brought forth many blessings to many people of the world.

You ask, "Did God make a mistake in allowing the previous pregnancy?"

No, humans make the mistakes, and God must rectify those and bring forth His perfect plan of action. God's plan is always perfect, and nothing, not even Coumadin, can stop what He has planned. I praise God for Jay Jay and for His perfect plan.

$\mathcal{A}$ Child to Love

"And a little child shall lead them."
—Isaiah 11:6

There was a time in my life when I almost made the most devastating of all mistakes—that being, I considered aborting my pregnancy, killing my child. There had been a lot of turmoil in my life and despair due to a most serious illness that attacked my husband. We had now been living with this debilitating disease for quite a while, which caused friction between us and a lot of unhappiness. As my husband and I realized what was ahead, we discussed what course we should take in our marriage. He did not want the children and me to have to see him gradually become worse or to cause us embarrassment of any sort. He would at times no longer hold up his head; he would stagger and fall, and would drool uncontrollably. He felt defeated, and his manhood was indeed diminished.

I was dealing with this, but his outbursts and anger became something of real concern. As this became worse and uncontrollable in most cases, we decided to separate and try to go our separate ways. Perhaps, in time, something new would be discovered that could help him. The lack of the stress of it all could be the answer.

He was always there for me and the kids when we needed him, and never missed a support payment nor failed to supply any other need we had. He was just there for us emotionally and in all other ways, as well. He loved us dearly and wanted to give us the best of everything. After a good six months, we decided to divorce and did so, and tried to move on with our lives, but the children were most unhappy and really missed their dad. The divorce became final, and we held onto each other and both cried, wondering if this was indeed the best for everyone. We certainly were not happy, the kids were miserable, and Richard felt lost when one of the episodes hit him. Thirty days passed and we knew this was a big mistake, and decided to reconcile our marriage.

During this time, I had found a new house that I wished to buy and contracted to purchase it. The old house was sold immediately. The deal was quickly closed, and

45

we moved into the new neighborhood and our new home. It was shortly after that that Richard and I decided to remarry, much to the joy of the children. The illness was in remission. Everything appeared to be good. We were again in church, and our friends were more than supportive, as was all the family. My family always loved and accepted Richard as one of theirs, and were very hurt when we divorced. Everything seemed to be really good, and we were happy.

As we moved into the beginning of summer, we received a shock when my stepfather suddenly passed away. This was difficult to receive at this time. He had been quite an influence in our lives, and the kids loved Pops dearly. I remember that we were getting dressed to go to the funeral in Gainesville, Georgia, when I really began to feel queasy. Nevertheless, we decided to go, which would be about a two-hour drive. Later, I became very nauseated and had to stop the car to throw up on two occasions. We continued on with our trip, but I really did not feel well at the funeral and had a recurrence on the way home.

Understand that I was now thirty-eight years old, and in those days it was not advised to get pregnant at this late age. I almost knew for certain that this was what was going on, but shared it with no one. My sister was expecting her child in August, and this was in May, so I felt sure we were going to both be having babies very close to each other. The latter part of June, it looked more certain, and I decided to make an appointment with the obstetrician.

You guessed it: I was indeed pregnant, and not happy about it at all. I told the doctor I could not be pregnant, that my husband was seriously ill, and I already had two children that I was concerned about raising alone. "No, I do not want to be pregnant!" I cried.

So, you ask, where is the miracle? A miracle indeed: Dr. Reilly had delivered my son, and my first child was delivered by his partner, so this was a medical practice that I knew well and trusted. I will never forget what followed my outcry. As I relay this to you, the miracle unfolds.

I had been ushered into Dr. Reilly's office to receive this unwanted news, and I sat on the other side of his desk as he delivered what he assumed would be joyful news and a real blessing for me. He glared at me in shock as I insisted I wanted to terminate my pregnancy. Without a word, he got up from his desk, excused himself, and told me, "Wait here."

I sat alone in the office for some twenty minutes, and again the door opened and he came back in. He did not look at me at all; his eyes were focused on the floor, and he proceeded as if I were not even there. Then, he once again arose from his desk, came to where I was, pulled up a chair in front of me, and glared into my eyes. His very blue eyes appeared as though they were going to pop out, and he began, "Mrs. Zubiena, this practice has not, and does not, and never will perform an abortion. We deliver babies to blessed families who want them, and will care for them, and love them. We don't kill them."

He then, after a long pause and a deep breath, now with a gaunt, almost angry look on his face, continued by saying, "Last summer, my wife attended a seminar at the First Baptist Church in Atlanta. When she came home, she was radiant, and told me about a young women who was in the group she had been put into. She went on and on about this young woman and her love for Jesus, and how it glowed all over her face. She added, this young woman is one of your patients. I asked who, and she said, 'Her name is Revonda Zubiena.' The way my wife talked about you so blessed me that I, too, wanted that kind of relationship with Jesus."

As he continued to look me in the eyes, those very blue eyes teared and he said, "Billie and I became closer because of that young woman's testimony." Then, with a mostly sorrowful and sad tone, he said, " I will not do your abortion. I will give you a name if you choose to do this, but I truly believe that that fetus will no sooner be out of your body than you will be crying for it." With that statement, he handed me a slip of paper with a name and phone number, and shaking his head, walked out of the room.

I went home that day and confronted my husband with the decision I had made. He began to cry and beg me not to kill our child. My heart was very heavy as he began to pray and beg his Lord to help him. Holy Spirit intervened here and touched my heart, and the pregnancy was continued.

Through Christmas was difficult, as the family were all excited, and with the family Christmas party, I made it; I sufficed without anyone being the wiser. My relationship with Richard was stressed, but we put on a happy face and made it through.

Finally, the day arrived. I was awakened by my water breaking. I knew the day was here for sure. I had the bag packed and bassinet ready. I had been given many showers, so everything I needed was in place. I knew I was in labor, but I was angry with Richard, so I allowed him to go on to work without telling him. As the contractions increased, I called my next-door neighbor, and they got me to the hospital and took care of the kids. They also called Richard, so he came to me immediately.

The birth was without complication and very fast. I was now the mother of a beautiful little girl. I kept telling the nurses I felt bad, so not to bring the baby to me yet. After more than a half a day, they pretty much got the message that I was rejecting my child, and all the more pushed her on me. Richard was bewildered. He thought that everything would change when she was born, but it had not changed at all. I still did not want her.

As evening came, the head nurse and the nursery nurse brought her in for me to feed her. I wanted to throw up, but I took her. They left me with her, and I was alone. Little did I know that they were watching me closely from the door. As I looked at my baby, her little eyes appeared as pieces of black coal, they were so deep in brown color. I looked at her and I said, "I am sorry, little baby, but I don't want you and I don't love you."

With that, my child's eyes teared, and I heard a voice of the little baby say, "That's all right, Mommy, because I am going to love you." As I am writing this, I am in tears. It is so hard for me to relate this, even now that that baby is approaching the same age as I was then, and has four children of her own.

The days passed, and this baby did exactly what she had told me she would do: she loved her mom and wrapped her mom's heart around her little finger. She was everything a mother could ask for in a child. She was obedient, sweet, and she loved Jesus. She is a blessing indeed, a real miracle for my life, and a joy in my old age. God gave the increase, and our family was blessed and enriched because of Jenna.

As the years flew by, this was the little girl who tugged on my skirt when I was "dressing up" for dinner, and after seeing her mom with makeup on, looked at me with total adoration and said, "Mommy, you look just like a clown." To her, that was a compliment. Not so for me, but today those words are so precious to me whenever I tell that story.

This was also the little girl who, when the minister asked for the head of the household to come forward to be anointed as head of the family, neither Richard nor I would go forward; we were annoyed with one another that day. Jenna said, "If you won't stand up for our family, I will!" She walked up to the altar with all the men and stood to be anointed for her family.

And then, the day Richard died, she was with me. She asked for the little pan I used to bathe him in and bathed her dead father, shaved him, shampooed his hair, and put his teeth in his mouth, put on clean bedclothes, and dressed him. She said she could not allow the funeral people to take her daddy anywhere until he was clean and dressed. The funeral attendants waited, then she allowed them to come in and take him. My older daughter, who had questioned what Jenna was doing, commented, "Mom, that was Jenna's alabaster box."

Miracle, you bet she is, and was and will always be to me a special gift from God to me, and I will always cherish that gift and praise God for her. She is always that hug I need, that sweet encouragement when I am down, and most of all, she has indeed been a true source of love to me. She was the glue that held the family together in difficult circumstances, a real strength in times of trouble, a blessing as she trusted her God, a miracle indeed.

"And a little child shall lead them."

The Pancake Mix

"Therefore take no thought, saying, What shall we eat? or, What shall we drink? or, Wherewithal shall we be clothed? (For after all these things do the Gentiles seek:) for your heavenly Father knoweth that ye have need of all these things."
—Matthew 6: 31–32

It seemed that sometimes God had to really shake me up to make me see what He is able to do for me. This was the case in approximately the early eighties, when my family was dealing with the onset of my husband's disability. He had been employed for a while by one of the top auto manufacturers when he began having some physical problems. As we went from doctor to doctor to get assistance, he was told that he should and could continue to work. Then, the shocker, when his company suddenly told him after a small accident that he was not able to do his job. This started a real tug-of-war on just who was right. It also started a real rough time for our family. There was no income. The doctors would not sign disability papers, because they did not believe he was incapable of work, and the company would not allow him to work. After a long and difficult fight, he was finally awarded disability from his company.

I had now begun working for physicians, and though my salary was acceptable, it was not a lot. It covered necessities, but seldom was enough to cover all the utilities, house payment, and food. I felt that I really needed to secure my job, and began praying and searching for a way to enhance my position. Having previously been employed with an industrial clinic, I felt I could possibly use some of the tactics that were used to increase patient volume for my orthopedist.

At this time, my job with the orthopedist was to file and follow occupational injuries for workers' compensation. I would talk regularly with the heads of company medical departments, and this was my in. I decided to make appointments to go to the companies and meet and talk personally to these people. I explained my idea to my employers, who were willing to allow me to give it a try, and subsequently, an appointment was made with a large cosmetic company. The idea was to talk to them and attempt to persuade them to refer their on-the-job injuries, as well as employment physicals, to my doctors.

The day finally came for my appointment with the head nurse of the cosmetic company, and I was invited for lunch. When I arrived, I learned that this was the first Tuesday, and therefore, this was a prayer lunch with other employees who wanted to participate. I was thrilled and excited to be a part of this group. The lesson that day was on the scripture Hebrews 13:17, "Obey them that have the rule over you, and submit yourselves: for they watch for your souls, as they that must give account, that they may do it with joy, and not with grief: for that is unprofitable for you." I accepted this Word in my spirit and knew God meant this especially for me that day.

Our office had just hired an older woman with a lot of business experience, but little medical experience at all. She was a nice lady, but somewhat overbearing. She seemed skeptical of me, and for some unknown reason had a lack of trust in me. She had been placed as my immediate superior, and it was not too good at this point. I read the scripture often, and asked God to give me the grace to be able to deal with her until I could come into her good graces.

As before stated, I handled all the insurance claims, both medical and worker's comp, and it was my job to keep up with the timely handling of these claims. My superior was in charge of all accounts for patients, and felt that this was her "domain." Sometimes these would cross over, and that was where the problem came into view. She did not want me discussing an account with any patient, and I certainly would oblige her rule.

A patient came by on this day and asked if her insurance had been filed, and when. It was always posted on the account card as to date filed, and subsequently was marked when paid. So, therefore, I would have to pull the card out of the account file to see what was notated. This was the only reference and the only way I could answer my patient's request.

I walked over to the account file to pull the transmittal card. My superior immediately assumed that I was going to discuss the account with the patient. She was overcome with outrage and anger, and walked up to me, jerked the card out of my hand, and slapped my face. I was terribly shocked, as was the rest of the office personnel. It became so silent you could hear a pin drop. The patient who was asking for assistance was in disbelief. They all thought there was indeed going to be a catfight right then and there.

I regained my composure, and turned and walked into my office area, immediately retrieving my *Christian Worker's New Testament*, and turned to the above referenced scripture. I asked for God's help and trusted Him to avenge me.

My superior went to the window where the patient was still standing in shock and asked if she could be of assistance. The patient shook her head and said, "No, you can't help me with anything." The patient then left. Everyone returned to their work, and that was that. I did not try to explain; I just sat still and allowed God to handle it. Of note, my superior did not apologize nor ask for any explanation. The doctors were told by other employees, but I said nothing.

I want to say something here: this lady was a born-again Christian, a big worker in her church.

My superior had set another rule, and that was that no one was to come into the office ahead of time to work, nor stay afterward. She felt that it was compromising, and no one should be in the office unsupervised. Of course, I was the only one who lived a distance away, and the only one, according to traffic, to sometimes got there ahead of any others. So again, this was primarily her distrust of me.

Unfortunately, when I arrived at home that night, I found my youngest daughter with high fever. I called to request coming into the office early so as to get her into the pediatrician. I would take her to the pediatrician and get a throat culture, and come back to the office to await my husband to take her home. She said that she would be in the office early anyhow, because she was going to a funeral and had to set up the charges before leaving.

When I arrived at the office, she had a stuffed animal for my little girl and then requested me to comb and put her hair up for her. She said she did not have time to get into the beautician and would greatly appreciate me doing this for her. I was cordial and agreed to do this, which I did. She insisted on paying me eight dollars, because she said that is what she would have had to pay her hairdresser. I took the eight dollars and left for the pediatrician's office. The throat culture was three dollars, and that left five dollars, of which a little more than half was used for a kid's meal. That left two dollars. Richard said there was a can of tuna at home which he would make for himself.

To go back a bit, it would be two weeks before I would get another paycheck, and we had exhausted almost all the food in the house. I did have some chicken parts, some broccoli, and a little butter. We made it through the dinner meal. I would now try to do something for breakfast the following morning. To add to the stress, my husband said, "I called the plant this morning and my check will not be in until Monday or Tuesday." It was Friday, and I was holding my breath.

It was now Saturday morning and the children were whining, "I'm starving!" I told them we would have to wait until the postman came, because I did not have but two dollars. Well, you know kids have no concept of money, and started to protest, "You have two dollars," as if two dollars would feed the world. I told them to pray, because if Jenna's culture was strep, the two dollars was for our insurance copay for her prescription.

We sat and waited. I went to the cabinets and moved everything around, and there was nothing but a can of cream-style corn. My kids did not like cream-style corn, and certainly not for breakfast. We waited. It was as if we could all hear the battery-operated clocks ticking louder and louder. Then, the phone rang. When they heard me give the pharmacy number, their faces dropped and they began to cry.

I had another complaint, this time from Richard, insisting he should call his dad and have him wire us some money. I insisted, "No, we are going to wait until the postman comes."

Earlier that morning my friend Pat had called and asked if I wanted to go to the grocery store with her. It seemed that Kroger was having the two-for-one sale, and she stated she always did better there when she had just a little bit of money. I told her I would have to pass, because my money was too little to help. We laughed and she said she understood. I was again having problems keeping Richard from calling Dad for money.

I prayed and said, "Lord, you know I trust you, and I know the postman is going to bring us relief, so help me here to hold Richard off."

I felt the Lord say, "Look in the cabinets again."

I said, "Lord, you know I already looked."

He said, "Look again."

Well, I looked at the little faces at the table and Richard's big puppy-dog eyes, and I said, "God says to look in the cabinets again." So, they watched as I moved everything around, and much to my shock, there it was: a package of pancake mix! Surely, this had not been there before.

The kids were jumping up and down, and Richard was in tears. How exciting it was to find a pack of pancake mix! I put on the griddle and took out a mixing bowl. When I emptied the package, I read the instructions on the back. It said, "Add one egg and one cup of milk."

I said, "Oh, God." I certainly did not want the kids to see my disappointment. Then, my God, as plain as could be, said, "Put in a cup of water and I will supply the egg, just beat it up fast."

Of note, I had a little butter and some syrup, but nothing else. I reached for my little hand mixer, turned it on high, and beat the mixture up fast, as directed. This made beautiful, big pancakes, enough for all of us to have as much as we wanted and none left over. As God provided the manna for one day, like so he provided the meals, one by one.

Then Richard said, "That's breakfast, but there is nothing for lunch."

I insisted, "Wait for the postman."

The children were watching for the postal cart to come, and here it came. Usually that postal cart casually rolled down the street very slowly, but not today. Not only did it not stop at our mailbox, but it "flew" by. That was the last straw for Richard. He said, "I am calling Dad."

I felt heartsick. I began to apologize to God. I said, "Lord, we have no choice. It's the children, we have to feed them." So, we called Dad and decided that instead of having him wire the money, we would have him call his bank and transfer funds into our account, and it would be there immediately. So, we gave him the routing number and bank account, and felt a little relief about the whole situation. I felt guilt.

We went back downstairs and began to make out a grocery list, feeling that money would be in the bank and we could buy for lunch and dinner for at least a few days until the disability check came. While figuring out what we had to have, the doorbell rang. Scot went to the door, and there was my friend Pat's son with two bags of groceries. He told us there was another bag in the car.

I immediately went to the phone and called my friend. I said, "Pat, what are you doing? I know you didn't have much money. How could you do this?"

She replied, "Well, not too long after you and I talked, I heard the postman blowing his horn. When I went out, I had a check in the mail for one hundred dollars. When I looked at it, God said, 'Roni needs half of this,' so when I went to the store, I bought one for me and one for you, exactly half."

My God says not to worry about what I will eat or drink, because he knows my needs and will supply them to me. You see, I thought Pat had enough, and if I had received the check I would maybe not have shared, but she was faithful to Him and God used her to supply our needs.

This is a beautiful miracle from God, but there was another part of the story. First, right after Dad hung up the phone, it rang again. His sister was being rushed to the hospital with a heart attack, which did take her life. Dad was very upset and needed to go immediately to the hospital to attempt to see her. He completely forgot to transfer the funds for us. We did not trust God, even though he had already fed us, but trusted man. God was faithful and supplied our needs, and Dad, in his grief, failed us. What a lesson we learned that day.

Now, for the second part of the story. My superior went home after the funeral that day, and there was an intruder in her home. She was terribly frightened and became depressed. She was in fear now to live alone and so depressed, she was referred to a therapist. She was prescribed some medication that did something to her thyroid and caused her to be completely unable to function at all. It took some weeks for her to recover, and during that time I was asked to perform her duties for her, which I did. After that, we became great friends and often talked about what the Lord had taught us through that unfortunate situation. When my daughter became old enough to marry, I called and asked her to direct Jenna's wedding. She was already booked up, but we felt a great respect for one another.

I have never tried to do the same thing again with the pancake mix, because I do not want to question God in His wonderful gift to us. My children remember what happened that day, and often, I am sure, when trials come, they remember, too, God is our provider, not man. His ways are miraculous and always done in perfect love.

To Him be the glory.

Joyce's Rooster

"Jesus saith unto him, Thomas, because thou hast seen me, thou hast believed; blessed are they that have not seen, and yet have believed."
—John 20:29

I was born in the city, raised in the city, and both my sister and I were never taught anything about country things. We knew our granny had chickens in her backyard and a number of different fruit trees, but as for farm living or country things, we were both as ignorant as could be. Having said this, you can just imagine how difficult it was for my sister, Joyce, to do farming. Granny always allowed us to collect the eggs from her three hens, and we had seen her, though regrettably, wring a chicken's neck to prepare it for Sunday dinner. This was the extent of our knowledge regarding chickens. She did have a rooster, though. That rooster would crow every morning at dawn, and this was a memory that stayed in Joyce's mind. This was the very thing that convinced Joyce that she just had to have a rooster.

Joyce and her husband had purchased a piece of property that had been used for some farm animals, and Joyce felt she wanted to have a farm. Well, a really good garden was plowed and sown, and then she decided to buy a goat. Next on her list was a few chickens, and she looked forward to getting fresh eggs in the morning. In the town where the "farm" was located, was the middle of the chicken business, with chicken farms going up all over everywhere.

Now was time for Joyce to get her chickens. She went to a little store near Fairmount and talked to the people there, who sold her six White Leghorn baby chicks. She was instructed on how to keep them until they were a little older, and she became mama chick to these little ones.

The chicks were about teenagers, and Joyce proceeded to build a hen house and fence to release her chicks into. They were safe and happy, and grew very rapidly. Certainly, they were well within the age to give eggs. But, there were no eggs! When she went down to the local store to find out what was wrong with her hens, she was surprised to learn that she had to feed laying mash. So, Mama Joyce began laying mash, and soon the eggs began to flow, and fresh eggs every day was a true blessing.

The next step was to have more babies to increase her flock. She wanted the hens to sit on some of the eggs, and left some in the nests to facilitate this, but much to her surprise, no chicks, just rotten eggs. Once again, Joyce went to the little store, where she learned "You can't have baby chicks unless there is a dad, Mrs. Wilson." It was necessary to have a rooster to make baby chicks. Now you know just how knowledgeable she was. Certainly, she really wanted a rooster now, but not just any rooster; she wanted a Rhode Island Red rooster.

She searched the area to see if anyone had any Rhode Island Reds, to no avail. She called all the local stores, and no one knew of anybody who even had a Rhode Island Red chicken. Well, she built a nice fence and hen house for her six chickens, and people in the area got a real kick out of Joyce and her chickens. Most everyone else in the area had a hundred or more, but Joyce was pleased with what she had, and soon, when she got her rooster, she would have more.

Later in the summer, she had an opportunity to go to a large flea market in Alabama, and you guessed it: there was her rooster. Right there in front of her in a special tent, roosters were for sale. Joyce did not know about what some of these roosters were purchased for, and did not even question the large spurs on this one. He was a handsome, large Rhode Island Red rooster, and quite a find, to say the least. They even had a cage for her to take him in.

He was not a happy rooster, being put in that cage and carried around all over the flea market. He often tried to attack through the bars of the cage. Joyce, being the softhearted person she was, felt so sorry for the rooster, and insisted, "Bless his little heart! He is just scared to death." She talked to him softly and told him how happy he was going to be in her big fence and with six beautiful hens. She encouraged him all the way home and could not wait to let him loose into the chicken yard. She decided to name him Thomas, because he was doubtful. Thomas, he was, and doubtful, he was not. He knew exactly what he intended to do, and there was no doubt in that.

Joyce was thrilled over this big boy. He had a marvelous cone on his head, and he was indeed a handsome bird. They had arrived home, and she placed the cage inside the fence just in case he chose to run. Carefully, he was placed in the middle of the fenced area with the other chickens. Now was the time. Joyce could hardly wait. Then, the door of the cage was lifted.

A gunshot could not have started a race faster than that rooster ran out of that cage. He immediately began attacking the hens, and they were squawking and Joyce was screaming. He was trying to kill her hens, and there was nothing she could do. Her son-in-law, Tom, came on the scene and rushed into the chicken yard and grabbed the rooster, who flogged him and cut his arms with those spurs.

Finally, Thomas was back in his cage. With this, Joyce said to the rooster, "You act like this and you will end up in the soup pot!" What in the world would she do about this rooster? Well, I will tell you what she did: she prayed over him. She told the Lord that she had asked for this rooster, and He had given him to her, and now she was asking Him just how to handle this rooster.

They left him in the cage overnight, and Joyce was looking forward to hearing him crow in the morning. Well, he crowed all right: at midnight, at one o'clock and two o'clock, and all night long he crowed, and no sleep was gotten by anyone, because of the crowing rooster. Joyce was sick at heart. She had fallen in love with that beautiful red rooster, and now she just might have to get rid of him.

The days passed, and she would go into the fence and pour feed just inside the cage. He would flog the side of the cage, and she had to be careful not to get cut by those big spurs. Each day, she told him that God was going to take care of him and help him to feel at home. You would think that rooster understood every word she spoke to him. He would cock his head and look at her, and make some noises as if to say, "You just think so! Just wait 'til I get out of this cage."

Well, he was not allowed out of the cage. Two weeks passed, and he was taking food from her fingers and she talked to him more. She prayed over him every day and told him God loved him and wanted him to be a good boy. Finally, her son-in-law, Tom, promised to come back over and they would allow him out again. This time, Tom was prepared, and Joyce had put the hens up in the hen house.

So, Thomas was allowed out. He walked around the yard, pecking the ground and holding his head high. No one was allowed in the fence but Joyce. After about a week of this, the door of the hen house was left open. To begin with, he ran them back in, but gradually they were able to come out and walk around with him. He was in charge, and you could see that readily. Thomas began to bring those hens into submission. When Joyce brought the food, Thomas scratched it and examined it thoroughly before he allowed the hens to eat. Then, he would stand back and allow them to eat. It was as if he was checking to make sure the food was okay before he allowed them to eat.

As Joyce watched carefully to see how he responded to the hens, she noticed a strange phenomenon. It seemed that somehow he had separated the hens and made them have their own nest. He somehow got the message to them that they could only go into their own nest. If they got into one of the other nests, he would run them out and make them go to their own nest. This was amazing. Neighbors came by to see this rooster perform "king of the hill," so to speak.

Also, he would not allow the hen to eat until she produced an egg. When she would cackle and have an egg, he would allow her to come eat. Without the egg, he would chase the hen back into the hen house. I don't know anything about chickens, but that seems a little farfetched to me, but it was true and proved over and over again. He also now only crowed at dawn. Thomas was a most wonderful rooster.

You may ask, "Where is the miracle?" Well, Thomas was a miracle. You see, Thomas had been trained to be a cockfighting rooster, and God had transformed him into a top-notch head-of-the-flock rooster. He became quite humble, and later on allowed the grandchildren to gather the eggs, but no one tried to pet Thomas; he was just not a petting rooster. He was all business, and he kept a tight ship.

Thomas was attacked one night and sustained a broken leg. My brother-in-law made a splint and splinted that broken leg, but Thomas could not stand on his perch. Finally, many years later, just parts of Thomas were found. Evidently, a wild animal felt he was a good meal, and that was the end of Thomas. My sister never again got another rooster. No one could compare with Thomas, but the story of this wonderful rooster has been told to bless many.

In the Book of John, Thomas is described as a doubter in Chapter 20: 27–28: "Then saith he to Thomas, Reach hither thy finger, and behold my hands; and reach hither thy hand, and thrust it into my side: and be not faithless, but believing. And Thomas answered and said unto him, My Lord and My God." Like so, Thomas the rooster was a doubter, but when prayed over, he became a believer and was transformed from a fighter gamecock to a keeper of the barnyard and protector of the inhabitants.

Joyce said, "That rooster represents a lot of us. We were all just that nasty when Jesus chose to die for us. Thomas's life changed because of the prayers which were prayed over him, and like so are we changed when we allow Jesus in our hearts." The miracle of God's mercy and grace is all sufficient. God shows us in His Word that life through Him is a changed life, and though we see Him not and still believe, we, too, become a miracle of His grace, as did Joyce's rooster.

Death Jump

"Thou shalt not tempt the Lord thy God."
—*Matthew 4:7*

There was a time in my life when I became unemployed, and it was very necessary that I have a job. My husband had been laid off his job due to being ill, and we were awaiting disability benefits. This was a long and drawn-out process, and our literal existence depended on my paycheck. I was able to get a temporary position with an orthopedist, but when that time ended, I once again was looking for work.

I had enjoyed an especially good working relationship with my temporary employer, and he was trying to find me another place to work. Finally, one of his colleagues called and knew of an opening at a psychiatric hospital in my area. Though a long drive from home, it was closer than the previous employer, so I went for an interview. After stating my salary requirements, I was told that they could not hire me for that much money. I went home wondering what was next . . . but not for long.

I received a call to come back in to be interviewed by the chief of staff, for whom I would be working. After the interview, I was taken back into the human-resources department and told I was hired. I later learned that my future boss insisted on hiring me even if he had to supplement the salary. He became a good friend and a wonderful boss over the next four years.

I worked as secretary. This included making appointments, doing the simple bookkeeping, and medical transcription. I also did a lot of personal assistance to him. I would go up to the units to check on his patients, and became well known and respected by staff and patients, as well.

There was no policy in place that forbade me from talking to the patients about Jesus, so I did just that. My boss had lost his only son to a drunk driver several years prior, at which time he leaned heavily on God and church. I put it in these words, because he believed in and relied on but did not adhere to the principals and standards of Jesus. He was not born again, but kind of on the fence, so to speak. So, I had, as his secretary, full support when speaking to someone about Jesus. It was in this context that the miracle I speak of here occurred.

His name was Levi, Jewish by birth, and son of a wealthy Orthodox Jew father. He was admitted to the alcohol-and-drug treatment program after being arrested and convicted of possession and trafficking of cocaine. My boss was up for the rotation, and therefore assigned Levi as our patient. It was many days before I met and spoke to him, but I was immediately drawn to him when I did have that opportunity. He was a very handsome young man in his late twenties, shorter than most men, but nevertheless tall enough. He had wonderful, unusual blue eyes, dark hair, and dimples. He spoke with a very strong, assertive voice, and immediately commanded respect. A little cocky, but likable, and certainly to all the young women, a real looker. I knew right away he was going to be a tough nut to crack, so to speak. I just spoke softly to him, and on every occasion I had, I told him God loved him.

As the days passed, it was finally visitation day. He had come far enough into the program that he was allowed to have visitors. It was during this time that I met his lovely young girlfriend. I noticed that he was wearing a cross around his neck this day, and later I had the opportunity to question it. He told me that she was a Christian and brought him the cross to wear. He certainly did not get the purpose of it. He did not know this Jesus it represented. Wow!

"God, are you giving me an entrance to this young man's life?" I questioned. Several days later, his brother, David, was admitted. It appeared that he, too, had a drug problem, but no legal problems related to it, so Dad brought him in, hopefully to keep him from getting into trouble.

David was a humble, quiet young man, and not affected by Levi's behavior. He was a good brother and sincerely wanted Levi to "get well." He introduced me to his dad on that day. Dad was a loving dad and very worried about his boys. He shared that they had lost their mother the previous November. I learned later that she, too, had a drug problem, and had taken her own life.

This man needed Jesus in his life very much. Well, you can just about guess what happened next: I told him *I* would be there for his boys, and that my Jesus would be there, too. Whoops! As I attempted to share Christ with this man, his face became more and more red. I was sure his blood pressure must have topped two hundred or more. With strong restraint, he asked me to hush. He was a Jew and did not believe my hogwash. Talk about adding fuel to the fire! I was on a roll. I quietly walked away, but I knew now these boys had to be given some hope.

The days seemed to be flying by, and time was of the essence now. I had only a few days left to share Christ with these young men, and with every breath I was in there pushing. I brought them tracts and devotionals, and with every opportunity I prayed for them and encouraged them to trust in Jesus.

The day before their dismissal came, their dad was in my boss's office. I thought he was there for instruction, but not so. He was there to file a complaint against me. He spoke with anger and no uncertain words. He wanted me fired, or else he would sue the facility. He felt that I had violated his paternal rights by talking Jesus to his sons. I was warned not to speak to them, and I was reprimanded by my boss, and that was that. I obeyed. Both completed their programs and were dismissed for home. I could only hope that perhaps something I had said to them would stick in their minds.

Some weeks later, at about 3:00 a.m., I received a call at home. It was the switchboard operator at the facility. She stated that Levi was on another line and was insisting to speak to me. I gave her permission to patch him through to me. I did not give out my phone number. He was crying and pleading for help. He was in New York and had purchased some black-tar heroin. I talked with him for a while and convinced him to give the drugs to someone who was there with him. He wanted me to allow him to come back to the facility. He was desperate.

I signaled the switchboard operator, who came on the line, and I explained what I wanted her to do. She, in turn, plugged in the admissions clerk for bed instruction, and all was set up. Levi was told to board the plane and we would have a van waiting at the airport to bring him to the facility. My boss was called and made aware of the arrangements and Levi's request that we not contact his father as to the goings on, and all was okay. Levi spent another two weeks and was dismissed to a halfway house.

It was now the last of November, the day after Thanksgiving. The autumn was moving in, and the days seemed to be getting shorter and colder. I was busying myself with my house and clean-up from the family get-together the day before. I had resigned my position at the facility to care for my sick husband. Once again, the switchboard operator called me. She said she had a phone call for me; the gentleman was requesting my phone number. When I inquired who it was, I was told it was Levi's father. I asked if she could patch me through, but was told she could no longer do that. I allowed my phone number to be given to him.

Almost immediately, the phone rang. A very hysterical father shared the following. It seems that Levi had again gotten into the drug scene, and in an attempt to save his brother, David had taken the drugs and locked himself in their mom's former apartment. This was an apartment on the sixth floor of a luxury high-rise. Levi knew that David had the drugs, and he wanted them. In his state, he asked the person who lived in the apartment next door to allow him to look out the balcony. The person would not allow him in, so he went to the seventh floor and again asked for entrance to an apartment. He was allowed in and went out onto the balcony.

As stoned as he was, he thought he could jump from this balcony over and down to the sixth-floor apartment balcony where his brother was held up with the drugs. This was the same apartment exactly one year prior that his mother jumped to her death. The tenant related that to her horror, Levi stood on the wall surrounding the balcony and jumped toward the balcony below. He missed. He fell the equivalent of seven stories. His fall was broken by a utility shed that had been set up for renovation of the complex. Levi was alive, but critical and screaming for me.

Dad begged, "Will you please come? My boy needs you."

I said, "Yes, I will be there as soon as I can make it."

He said, "Please hurry."

I quickly dressed and asked my neighbor to take me there, because I did not know how to get to that hospital. When I arrived, I went straight to ICU, and they knew I was coming. I was ushered in immediately to a screaming young man—screaming in pain with vulgarity like never before heard. As I was brought into the room, I walked over to a nonhuman-looking cocoon body with all kinds of tubes and monitors attached to it.

In undescriptive horror, I spoke. "Levi," I said, "it is Roni. I am here with you."

With that, he stopped screaming and spoke my name over and over. I attempted to find a place that I could touch some skin. This was not possible. Every part of his body was covered. He had a fractured pelvis, both legs and both arms, and cracked vertebra, not to mention a concussion. Miraculously, he was alive.

I touched him, and began to pray and ask my Lord to be very real and present with him. He became calm. As the nurses stood in awe, Jesus moved in and took over. I quietly left the room and went to the waiting father. He hugged me so tightly, I felt I could not breathe. He said, "If your Jesus can do this, then perhaps I need to know Him."

I prayed with him and left the hospital for home. I checked on Levi regularly while he was in the hospital; however, I never spoke to him or his father again. I know that the nurses were amazed over his recovery, but also disgusted over his terrible behavior to the staff there. I never attempted to go back to the hospital. I had given this family to my God.

This is now 2010. The autumn is about to again come in and show off her vivid colors, and the air is becoming a little brisk in the mornings. Once again, my thoughts turned to this family and the many sorrows they faced. As of now, I have never again heard from any of the three, but I feel sure that Jesus and His angels have indeed taken them as their own. I feel sure if there had been any more problems, I would have been notified.

I was given the privilege of sharing in a most magnificent miracle. My God trusted me to share Him with this family. I pray that my God will be glorified as those who choose to read about this are blessed. We are warned not to tempt the Lord, and in this situation, God ruled supreme. I pray that they are now completed Jews and know Jesus to be King of Kings and Lord of Lords.

Pride and Joy

"How is it that ye sought me? Wist ye not that I must be about my Father's business?"
—*Luke 2:49*

I had wanted grandchildren for some time, but only now was that dream coming true. My sister had children older than my children and already had the joy of three grandchildren. It seemed it was never going to get here for me. Now, with extreme excitement, my dream was finally coming to be.

It was a very cold and dreary February night with ice and snow on the way, and my daughter began to have contractions. It was not quite time for the baby to come, but the contractions got closer, and since we lived a good fifty miles from the hospital and the weather conditions were worsening, we decided to go in for a check. Her regular doctor was out of town, so this doctor on call really encouraged us to come in, because he did not know the patient and could not assess the situation on the phone. We put everything together and loaded up to go on the treacherous route to the hospital. Finally, we arrived just as her water broke, so we were well on our way to having a baby. Our dad-to-be was called and came there with us immediately.

I had agreed to be her coach for birthing, but I really wanted Dad to be involved. Of course, I had an ulterior motive: I wanted him to be involved with the baby, knowing that he would gain a real acceptance and love. It was not long when I realized that with each contraction, something seemed to be wrong. I called the nurse and told her that I felt that there was something wrong. With every contraction, the baby's heart rate went down. They did not seem to be concerned, but I felt there was really a problem.

I watched and counted the beats until the contraction was over, at which time the baby's heart rate slowed to a near stop. I was frantic and insisted that the nurse call the doctor, who advised them to put another monitor and see if the present one was faulty. The new one had the same response on contraction. With this, they called the doctor back and were advised to place a fetal monitor inside the womb. Well, this indeed showed that with every contraction there was lowering of the heart rate of the fetus. The fetus was in distress.

The doctor was called, and my daughter was prepared for surgery. A C-section was set to be performed due to fetal distress. I prayed over my daughter and had prayed over my little grandbaby for all the time we were here. I knew this was to be a special child, the answer to my prayers, and I wanted him to be covered completely. My daughter had sat on the porch at night and any other time reading her Bible during the whole pregnancy, and read the scripture to this baby from the beginning. We had to trust that God would not only protect him in the womb, but as he was born.

The dad had finally arrived and was there on time to be with her for a few minutes, but I was the one allowed to go into the operating room with her. I stood, and watched, and prayed. When the opening was complete, the doctor reached in and asked about the monitor, which showed the heart rate was very slow. It was touch-and-go for a while. He was able to move the baby around enough to reveal the cord wrapped tightly around his neck, and though difficult, was able to be removed. He was brought out a little blue, but slowly returned to the pink that he was supposed to be. His Apgar scores were above normal and all was well. To stop the hemorrhaging of my daughter, I was asked to exit the operating room with the baby, and they worked to restore my daughter's blood supply, and eventually they came to report she was fine. She had apparently had a prolapse of the placenta, a very serious situation. We were told that we were lucky that we brought her in so soon.

"Not lucky," I said. "We are blessed."

The blessing was that when the pediatrician was called and came to check the baby, it was the pediatrician who was a wonderful friend for whom I had worked for several years. He was excited to see me and to see I finally had that grandchild I so wanted. He also added that I was indeed blessed to have the doctor who came to deliver him. The doctor was a born-again Christian and began praying for my grandbaby the minute he was called. He was also in God's hands while doing the surgery, and later told us of the extreme difficulty. This doctor gave God the glory.

My grandson became the light of my life, so to speak. He was everything I always wanted in a grandchild. He was obedient, smart, very good-looking, and he really loved his Mee Maw. That is all due to the constant input of the Word by his faithful mother. This child was spiritually filled from the beginning. He was always a child of God and is still today.

As I write this account, he just turned twenty-four years old. He was called of God into His service as a youngster. He started a gathering at his high school of young people who would meet at the flagpole every morning for prayer before entering school, and was known by his peers to be a Christian who followed Christ and His principles. He received the honor of "Star Student" for the county and went on to college. There, he earned a BA and MA at the same time, and graduated in the top of his class. Also, I failed to report, he received an associate's degree in theology while still in high school.

Am I proud of this grandson? You bet! I also recognize the miracle of his birth. I know that the enemy knew what this young man would become for the Lord, and was indeed trying to kill him in the womb. Prayer was the answer here, and pray we did. God continues to use Cory and the story of his birth and life. We do not know at this point where God will ultimately use him, but you can be assured that Cory is faithful to be about His father's business.

Miracle on the Highway

In the years of 1990 through July 1996, it seems that the Lord was really busy in my life. My mother had been diagnosed with lung cancer, and my husband, Richard, had had more frequent and more severe exacerbations of his MS. However, there were some real blessings that occurred. My faith had become more stressed, yet really a great deal more defined as to where I was in my relationship with Christ. I had been running from my husband's illness and was in total denial. I was hurt that God would allow me to go through this. I started misbehaving and being someone that both God and I knew I was not. I was trying "new" things unacceptable by Him and certainly, at any other time, would have been unacceptable by me. I was just an "I want" person, and my husband, feeling guilty for being so ill, just complied with my wishes.

The previous year, he had bought me my first horse, and at fifty years of age, I decided to learn to ride. My horse was an amazing animal: a silver-gray, purebred Arabian gelding. He was wonderful. He was so well-trained and sensitive to my every touch that I began to ride very well and very soon. As my teacher said, I was indeed a natural.

I was very happy to spend time with my horse, until one day this very spoiled woman saw, coming across the pasture, a real dream of a horse. In the afternoon sun, she was a lavender-colored filly that had the most magnificent "dish," and was about the most beautiful horse I had ever seen. I fell in love. She was feisty and cute, and she really liked me. I wanted that horse in the worst way.

I talked to Richard, and he said, "But, you have a horse. Do you want to get rid of him?"

Of course not! Son was my best friend right then. I spent all my time at the barn— that is, spare time, which I had very little, but he was my love. So, why another? I just really dreamed of my daughter Jenna, who was an excellent rider, learning to ride well enough to compete. It was quite an exciting thing to be involved with the Arabian competition. I wanted this magnificent horse and my daughter to be involved. So, the deal was made, and Samanda was now mine.

I was excited at the possibility of competing with well-known horses, and one of which was a sibling of Samanda and was winning lots of titles. To back up a bit, my oldest daughter did not ride and could not understand why I wanted to be around stinky horses. Certainly, her mother had never been the kind of woman to spend time at the barn. My youngest had had a paint horse given to her, and loved horses and rode extremely well, so at that time I was not alone in my pursuit. Kelli, my oldest girl, complained a lot about my time at the barn and thought I was just "disgusting." She had been going through a breakup with her boyfriend and had entered into a state of depression. I was quite concerned about her spending too much time alone and becoming more and more depressed. So, when Scot bought me "Samanda" shortly, Kelli again started her reprimand to me, and more so now that I had two horses, which, as she said, was "ridiculous."

Finally, on one of those days when Kelli was down in the dumps the most and angry with me about the horses, she came to the barn. She just wanted to see what was so wonderful about "that danged horse." Samanda's previous owner was blonde, about 5'7", and wore a specific brand of cologne. Well, you guessed it, Kelli, though not blonde, had a lot of sun bleach in her hair and wore the same kind of cologne. When Kelli went into the stall to speak to Samanda, the horse, smelling the cologne, thought Kelli was Janet, her previous owner. She began to follow Kelli, sticking her nose on Kelli's neck and nudging Kelli in a loving response. This about blew Kelli away. "Mama, look at this horse! She is following me everywhere I am going, and it's almost like she is trying to kiss me!"

Kelli was falling in love. The little filly had won her heart, and thus started a long summer of Kelli working with her. The depression cleared, and what a joyful girl she became. Miracle? Yes, of a sort, but this was only the beginning of what would come.

As the long, hot summer continued and we all enjoyed our horses at the barn, another miracle came along in the form of Ben. Yes, Kelli met the brother of one of the other girls at the barn. This started a long and exciting romance for Kelli. For a while, I thought perhaps Kelli would just spend time with Ben and forget about Samanda, but that did not happen.

On the front page of the *Marietta Journal* was the picture of a girl with her horse;

this was the overall winner of the Georgia Olympics. When the horse owner and some of the pedigree was listed, Kelli liked to have had a fit. That horse was a sister of Samanda. Now Kelli was on a roll; she could just see herself riding Samanda at the 1996 Olympics.

Immediately after this, Kelli contacted the other horse's owner and talked to her for some time. Then, she met a man who trained Hollywood celebrities' horses. Kelli bought all the horse magazines and began to research training. The name of an excellent trainer was given to her, and we found that the place this trainer worked was right in Alpharetta, Georgia.

Kelli contacted the trainer and talked to her about Samanda. The trainer was impressed with our credentials and offered to come to our barn to look at the horse. Well, as I said, Kelli had purchased all these horse magazines, and when she arrived at the barn, Ronald Reagan and the Shah of Morocco were shown with this particular trainer. It seemed that this lady was indeed a top trainer of the Arabian horses and promoted horse participation internationally.

We were looking for a horse to breed Samanda with, and this place had access to the best. So, we talked about this, but were advised if we wanted to compete, then we should put off the breeding for a while. Since Kelli was not that good a rider and the Olympic trials would be coming soon, we opted to take Samanda to Augusta to train with a top trainer there who would train the horse and Kelli at the same time. Thus set up the extraordinary miracle ahead: We would go every Saturday to Augusta and Kelli would spend almost a whole day working with riding techniques, dressage, and other figures, and Samanda was brilliant. She responded to every command and was very tight, and we were excited as to our outcome. But, this was not to be. We never would have guessed what came next.

This Saturday was not a good day. It was beautiful weather and the perfect day to ride, travel, and picnic—anything, a gorgeous day. Kelli evidently got up on the wrong side of the bed, I guess. Cory, my older grandson, and Kelli's son really did not want to go. He protested and pitched a fit, and his mother would have nothing else but that he would indeed go. I was not feeling well myself and tried to get her to pass on this day, but to no avail.

Finally, after a real knock-down drag-out confrontation, we got in the car to go. We had not gotten too far down the road when I received a call on my cell phone. This was from a friend who stated he had a bad feeling about the trip today. He pleaded with me and Kelli not to go; he just felt something bad was about to happen.

In the last of the conversation, he said, "Be especially careful with eighteen-wheelers." From that moment on, I began to pray, especially as we started to pass or be passed by one of the big rigs. However, our trip to Augusta was without incident, at least going there.

As we started back home, the traffic was very heavy: lots of big rigs and certainly lots of fast-moving traffic. As we approached the 285 loop, I insisted that Cory put his seatbelt on. He had been in the back seat, and I noticed he did not have the belt on. He complained and noted that I did not have my seatbelt on. He was right; I did not. I hated to put those things on, but knew I must if I was going to get him to. So, all seatbelts were in place, and Cory laid down in the back seat and shortly fell asleep.

As we came off 85 and onto 285, again I was moved to begin to pray. We came through the loop without incident, as we did on I-75, and I felt relieved. We were approaching the turn-off for Lockheed, and then were in the extreme righthand lane. In the lane beside us was a white eighteen-wheeler, who later advised that he thought we exited, but we did not; we were in his blind spot, and suddenly, out of nowhere, it happened. The large truck cab crunched into us and grabbed our fender, dragging the car down the expressway. Miraculously, when this happened, Kelli instinctively through the gear into neutral; we were free-moving with the truck.

Suddenly, realizing what was happening, the truck slammed on his brakes and we were thrown, spinning like the tilt-a-whirl at the carnival, spinning 'round and 'round up the highway. At the same time, I was covered by a great white light. I did not know where it was coming from. It was so bright, it blinded me to anything around. I was unable to see at all except for the extreme, brilliant-white light. I looked to try to find its source, but it was too bright for me to see anything but the light itself. And then, that voice I know so well, but not the quiet, peaceful voice that always spoke to me—this was almost angry, but certainly very sharp and stern: "Oh, no you don't! Not this way."

I looked up. We were headed across in front of a second eighteen-wheeler, and headed for the center concrete wall. When I say that, I knew instinctively that the other lane of traffic on the other side of that eighteen-wheeler would be heavy and directed right at us. We were in a Nissan Sentra, a very small, compact car, and I thought for sure we were goners.

At this point, I glanced at my daughter, who was temporarily unconscious, and I was at complete peace in my spirit. I said, "Here we are, Lord. I commit us into your care." I truly felt we would be killed.

There were no cars on the other side, but there was the wall, which we crashed into and bounced back into the path of the large red-and-white Peterbilt truck. The monster truck slammed on its brakes and did almost a cha-cha before hitting us again. We were hit on all four corners of the car, but no windows broken, and the passenger compartment was not compromised. The small car was totaled, and we came to a stop right back where the whole thing started.

Someone ran over to the car and shouted to the onlookers on the side of the road, "They are alive!" I, in turn, called 911 and asked for assistance, and soon ambulances and police were there on the scene. The eighteen-wheelers did not fare as well. They had to be towed away from the highway. I guess in this case, bigger was not necessarily better.

How could this be? Only God knows and only God controlled the situation. The blessings which followed were many, and we proclaim them today.

There was a small truck with a whole little league baseball team in the truck bed just in front of us as the accident began. Had we not been hit, that little truck with all those little boys may well have been the victims of a sleepy truck driver who was looking behind rather than ahead. We were used as a substitute. God protected us because of the prayers we had uttered all that day. I am still amazed at the light which surrounded me. I feel that it was truly the glory of God and His protection, and of certain, the voice that commanded the spirit of Satan away. What a miracle indeed, and so undeserved, but God is true, even when we choose not to be.

Forever, omnipotent, omniscient, and certainly sovereign is my God, and to Him be all the glory. He promised He would never leave nor forsake those whom He loves, and I know He loves me, and I trust Him for all things, both good and bad. He can use them to my good and to His glory.

Of note: Not only were there no windows broken, but there should have been a whole line of cars in the rush-hour traffic as we crossed over, but not even one car was there. The large Peterbilt hit us exactly with his bumper squared with the auto cross members, and pushed the car sideways. By rights, it should have crashed over this small car, but it somehow pushed us. The pavement was not wet; it should not have slid. We bounced off the concrete wall as if it were rubber. It took five hours for the trucks to be cleared from the highway, yet the passenger compartment of the small car was not violated at all.

Ryan, the Rescue Hero

"For he shall give his angels charge over thee, to keep thee."
—Psalm 91:11

Over the years, I have learned all about the cartoon characters due to my children and grandchildren watching TV. One of these cartoons showed stories about the heroes who come to our rescue: the police, firemen, and paramedics. These were some of the really special ones that my little grandchildren watched. They often pretended that they were the firemen and the policemen, and certainly were excited when they got the chance to see any of these heroes. This story begins with a real blessing that we as a family enjoyed so much.

After quite a long period of time in which we labored to get disability for my husband's long illness, we were finally blessed with receiving the benefits. It had been such a long time from the beginning that when the benefits were given to us, a very large sum of money was afforded us in back payment. We were able to enjoy some of the niceties of life, one being a swimming pool.

My children were now adults, and they enjoyed having the pleasure of swimming, and with my husband being ill, we seldom went on vacation. The backyard became the sole source of our entertainment. This pool had hosted many parties and luncheons, and ultimately became a baptismal pool for my grandson Cory to receive his baptism. We loved our pool, and certainly shared it with all who wished to partake of the pleasure.

My daughter had previously decided she wanted to go into the medical profession, and in order to begin this, she went to work right out of high school at a nursing home. She received training there to be a certified caregiver, and enjoyed her job. Some of the training was to give CPR. This also had been a requirement for her when she worked with disabled children, so she was well qualified to perform this, should the circumstances demand it. We did not know how important that training would be until many years later.

On Easter Sunday, my daughter came to church with me and brought her small children. That day, the little ones were told about Jesus and how He died for them in the Sunday school class. They were also told about angels, and how an angel told people about Jesus being born. The children, though very young, had colored pictures of angels and were impressed with these stories.

Several days after the Easter week was over, we were enjoying our backyard. It was too early to open the pool, and the cover was still on. Sometime earlier that week, there had been a storm that had a lot of wind, and it somehow dislodged the pool cover so that a corner was loose. I was not aware of this, but when my neighbor came over to sun on our pool deck, I had noticed this was the case.

Later that afternoon, my small dog kept crying and was trying to tell me something. I felt something was wrong, but could not put my finger on what it was. I remember telling my neighbor to move her lounge chair more away from the edge of the pool, because our bulldog had bad eyesight and I was afraid she would fall through the cover edge. Well, as Furbie continued to tell me something was wrong, I went to call Gertie, the bulldog. When she did not come, I went to look for her. I searched under the deck, under the shed, all around, and she was nowhere to be found. Finally, Furbie ran to the edge of the pool and seemed to give a signal. Gertie must have fallen into the pool.

I was frantic and called the young men who had moved into the house next door to come and help take the cover off. Sure enough, there was my bulldog, drowned in the pool. We drained the pool, retrieved the dog, disinfected, and refilled. I felt that to put the cover back on would be dangerous with the children, so it was left off. There was another cold snap, and still too cool to officially open the pool for swimming.

This was the following week. My daughter had come to my home with the two little boys—two years old and three and a half years old—and her new baby of six months. I had installed special chain locks on the doors, a gate on the back porch, and a chime on the door so as to protect the children from the pool. I was in my bedroom reading, and my daughter brought the baby upstairs to change her. I heard the chime on the door and felt sure she had gone back down the stairs. And, she heard the chime, but felt that I was down there. When she heard me cough, she went to see who went out the door.

The older child had climbed on a stool, unlocked the chain, and opened the door. Both little boys climbed over the gate and were in the pool area.

When my daughter walked through the kitchen, she looked out the window and saw Ryan leaning over the side of the pool, and immediately ran to the porch. She called out to him, "Ryan, get away from that pool right now!"

Ryan replied, "I can't! I have to get Eric."

My daughter said, "Where is Eric?"

Ryan replied, "In the pool."

Needless to say, my daughter screamed, and ran and jumped into the pool to get her child. He was not breathing and was blue-black, totally unconscious. I will never get that sound out of my memory as she screamed, "Mama, help! Call 911!"

I ran to the phone, and strangely enough, it was as if I had never before seen a phone. Suddenly, I did not even know how to use it. But, in what seemed to be forever, I did dial the phone and called 911. When the 911 operator answered, I told her that my grandson was drowned in the pool and to come quickly. At the same time, I was crying out to Jesus and screaming to Jenna to do what she knew how to do: CPR.

The 911 operator was trying to get information from me, but it was more important to me to continue to cry out to Jesus and give instruction to Jenna. Finally, Eric coughed, and water came from his nose and mouth, and he was breathing, but still unconscious. By this time, all my neighbors were coming from all directions, and the police, fire department, paramedics, and ambulance were here. They came in and took over, and we attempted to get some clothes on and get some towels and warm blankets for Eric.

The paramedics continued to check Eric out, and decided he would have to be taken to Scottish Rite Hospital for observation. The police officer began to ask about how this happened, and then talked to Ryan about what happened. Ryan said, "I climbed up on the stool and unlocked the door, and me and Eric climbed over the fence." He further stated that they were leaning over to blow bubbles in the water when Eric fell in. Ryan grabbed Eric's shirt when he came up and held onto it until his mom came out.

The paramedics said to Ryan, "You are really a rescue hero, and you were very strong to hold your brother."

Ryan replied, "No, I wasn't strong. The *angel* helped me to hold him."

This was the first time these children had been to Sunday school, and on that Sunday they learned about Jesus and angels. We never know just how much one encounter with the Lord can mean to a child. I believe—and so did the professionals who were on the scene—that Ryan was too small to have been able to hold his brother without help. Surely, there was indeed an angel who was there and answered the call.

One other thing of note: My daughter was screaming so much, she said she had no air to breathe into her child's mouth, but someone did, and Eric began to breathe.

It was noted that probably Eric had filled his lungs to blow the bubbles and fell in with a full lung of air, and had Ryan not caught his shirt, deep water would have forced the air from his lungs, resulting in full-drown mode. Because he did not sink back to the bottom, his lungs were only partially filled, and therefore, he suffered no brain damage.

Today, Eric is about to turn twelve and his brother, Ryan, will turn fourteen in June. They both remember the events that took place and certainly agree that Ryan was indeed a rescue hero, only with the help of an angel.

The following day, I had the pool drained and filled in, and a beautiful prayer garden was put in its place. We are thankful to our God for the substitute of Gertie, which without her loss we could be today still suffering the consequences. This story was shared the following week in a packed church in Ball Ground, Georgia. Also of note: Not only was there no brain damage to Eric, but he is a straight-A student and quite the brilliant young man.

I hope that this story will encourage you to learn CPR and never trust locks or gates when it comes to pools and children. Only the personal, watchful eye will work, but know that in the event of trouble, Jesus will be there. Call on Him.

We are also thankful to the 911 operator who quickly got the rescue squad on its way, but she also cried out to Jesus with me, and we know where two or more are joined and are in agreement, God is always there in the midst. This 911 voice joined me in my urgent cry to Jesus and became the *two* with me that fateful day. May God's blessings be constantly upon those who are there to assist us when such emergencies come into plan. Thank you, Lord, for believers.

Translation Peace

"And the peace of God, which passeth all understanding,
shall keep your hearts and minds through Christ Jesus."
—Philippians 4:7

I was the caregiver of my husband, and it seemed that I just could not pull it together this day.

My mother had died from lung cancer, and it seemed the process took forever. She had insisted on surgery at my continued plea for her not to do so. She was eighty-three years old and had been extremely vital, able to work rings around me and able to take care of herself and my brother. I felt that surgery would only steal away the last years that she could live out happily. This was her decision, though, and we began to travel that long road of sickness, which did not lead to recovery. She was promised at least five years, but just short of one year, she was gone.

Many nights, I rested in my bed and talked to the Lord. Many of these nights, I taught out loud an imaginary class. Sometimes, when my son got up at 3:00 a.m. to go to work at the post office, he would look inside to see to whom I was talking. He would just shake his head and smile, as he knew I was either talking to God or to someone about God. Tonight was no different, and he gave a quick wave and was out the door.

As I laid there in my bed, I closed my eyes and felt the hand of my mother in mine. Mother had never been a real comfort to me. Not that she did not love me, but she was just not there for me in a sympathetic way. My husband had become bedridden, and now he was my patient and not the husband I loved so much. I am sure Mother cared very much. She certainly did love Richard, but her response to me was lacking. It was as if she just did not know what I needed from her.

So soon after her death, I felt her hand in mine. I spoke to her and told her I knew she was okay, and I thanked her for allowing me that revelation. I was awake, my light was on, and once again Scot peeped into the room and said nothing, just a smile and a quick nod of his head, then out the door to work, as always. Then, it happened.

I was suddenly somewhere else. I did not recognize where. It was like on a path, but a staging place of sorts. Suddenly, a young man dressed all in white said, "I have come to carry you home." I thanked him as he reached down to pick me up. As he raised me onto his shoulders, much like a child would be carried on her father's shoulders, I said, "No, no. I am afraid of heights."

In a very soft and kind voice, he said, "Just close your eyes and enjoy the ride."

I remember how I felt: no fear, just confusion at first. I did need a way to go home, but this was unusual, to say the least. I did as he said; I closed my eyes. I felt secure in his strong arms, and although he was not a tall man, I felt he was certainly capable of holding me safely. I could describe him as approximately 5'9" and maybe 150 pounds—not big, but strong. I don't remember looking into his eyes, so I do not know their color. Nor did I record his hair in my memory. I was just overtaken with his grace, and charm, and kindness. His voice was somehow familiar, but I could not place it. His all-white suit was well tailored, and he wore white shoes. Somehow, I felt I had met him before.

The journey began. With my eyes closed, I could feel a soft breeze against my face. My hair gently tossed in the air, and it seemed I was traveling in circles. Larger, then larger, and with each circle we went higher. Suddenly, I felt complete peace. There was no sound, only the gentle rustling of the breeze as it passed my face. I became lost in this feeling of peace and quiet, and we soared like an eagle through the air. I did not know my destination. I thought he was taking me home, earthly home, from somewhere that I did not know how I had gotten there.

Then, reality returned to me, and I said, "I think I better go back now." Immediately, as I spoke, we were back to natural surroundings, and he carefully took me off his shoulders and placed me on the ground. The moment that my feet touched the ground, I was back in my room in my bed. I closed my eyes, because I wanted that peace that passed all understanding again, but the trip had ended, and I was left with something I did not understand but knew was a miracle of peace.

I attempted to make sense of it all, but it was just too strange and wonderful. I don't know why I was given such a special treat. Perhaps a choice to escape my sorrow? I don't really know.

After I began to teach the Sunday school class, I was teaching the part of the New Testament that gave the account of the translation of Philip, and I recognized what I had experienced. I further wondered if the young man may well have been my daddy. Maybe just a chance to feel him as I had never been able to as a young child?

I don't know, but I do know I was not asleep when this happened, and I can still, in my memory, feel the soft breeze and hear his voice.

Today, now eighty-two years old myself, I recall these things and know that I was given a very special gift. Hard to believe, hard to understand, but it most definitely happened. A true miracle of my very own.

I say to you "that peace that passes all understanding" is worth the wait.

My God Is My Carpenter

*"Is not this the carpenter, the son of Mary, the brother of James,
and Joses, and of Juda, and Simon?"*
—*Mark 6:3*

I have always been one who enjoys building and doing those kinds of things about my house. My husband used to jokingly say to others that he would never come into the house in the dark for fear I had moved the wall. That was somewhat true, and I did indeed do a lot of things like that. I had really gotten to where I could do most anything as long as I could lift it, but there were sometimes when I really had a problem getting things to work. I prided myself in saying that I was a carpenter by trade, but in truth, I was a carpenter by God's ever-ready hand.

When we decided to put in a swimming pool in the backyard, I also wanted to have my deck enlarged to enhance the pool surround. My existing deck was somewhat high off the ground and not very accessible to the poolside. I decided I wanted to do a three-level deck, so that there would not be such long steps to get to the pool area.

I called in a couple of young men who needed work and described what I wanted done, and before long, there was the three-level deck, all done and ready to enjoy. The top was the existing deck, and then there were just seven steps to another deck the same length and width as the top deck. Off that area was a one-step stepdown, and then three long steps to the pool surround. It looked quite amazing when it was finished. I had it painted a beautiful medium-blue and trimmed with bright-white bannisters and rails, and it was indeed quite striking.

I noticed that when standing back away from the deck, though, I could see straight under the deck and all the pool works, and the air-conditioning system, and all that was not attractive at all. I tried to distract from it by using very large pots planted with multiple petunias of all colors, and this looked good, but still, there were those places where you could still see the ugliness of the equipment.

I studied this for some time and finally decided to buy some lattice to cut and place into the areas. I fashioned it in such a way that I could lift up one section to easily access the pool pump and controls. All that was needed now was to figure how to get them in place and without help. That could pose a problem.

I went to the home-improvement store and purchased the all-white Teflon lattice. It would not require painting and was guaranteed for twenty years, so that would be just the thing to use. I had it loaded up on the top of the van and tied down, and now it was at home. My son kindly obliged me by lifting it off and placing it in the backyard to make it easy for me. I talked to him about helping me with this project, but having to go to work at 3:00 a.m., he was hardly ready to do this for me when he got off in the afternoon. He did not refuse to do it; it just never seemed to be getting done.

I was having a problem getting anyone to cut it to size for me, and it seemed it was never going to be finished. I had been stung by having some young fellows doing my previous work, and when I paid them in advance, they just never came back and finished the work. I did not feel that I could pay for it again, and then, too, this was something I felt that I could do myself.

The second-level deck was approximately thirty inches off the ground, so I just put that lattice down on it and stood on the ground, and using my handy saber saw, measured and cut all of it myself. That is, with the guidance of that special carpenter I so often call upon.

It was all cut to size and ready to be installed. There was no problem with the pieces that went next to the ground; they just stood in, and I used sheetrock screws and attached it to the posts, and all was well. It looked wonderful and became a backdrop for my beautiful pots. Now to attempt to install the second-level pieces.

I went around under the top deck and pulled the sheets of lattice under to be closed. I was ready to attach them when I realized I could not hold up a whole sheet of lattice and apply the screws, as well. I tried several times to put in the first corner screw, but the angle of the lattice would not fit in so as to be held in place. I then tried to stack some paint cans to prop the lattice against, but that did not work. Because of its flexibility, it just would not stay. I tried everything practical that I could think of, and finally, I sat down and cried. I was really having a "pity party," and was more than complaining that I did not have anyone to help me. I cried out to God and asked him why it was, at this age in my life when I really needed a husband, I was unable to have him to help me.

After I had cried myself out and there was no one to comfort me, I bucked up and tried again. Still, it would not work. Then, that still, small voice I know so well said to me, "Put the bottom corner in first, and it will hold until you can pick up the top and screw it in." What I had made so difficult was made absolutely simple and easily done very quickly. I wondered why I didn't think of that first. It certainly would have saved me a lot of heartache and trouble. But, I just had to complain, and as you know, God says in Philippians 2:14–15, "Do all things without murmurings and disputings: That ye may be blameless and harmless." He wants us to trust Him in all situations, and when we do and have faith in Him, all things come together exactly as they should.

The underpinning was complete and looked beautiful. All who came by could not believe that I could have possibly done it myself, but I stood tall and proud, but certainly I had to say I had a specialist to help me all along. I had God as my carpenter, and He was an expert. After all, look what He did with all the world around us.

It was quite a thing after that, when many of my friends called me over to help them to do projects that they could not figure out how to do. The Lord and I trained a lot of housewives in the art of doing these things before their husbands got home. Fortunately, none ever resented or faulted me for the projects we did, but were thrilled that their wives were doing some of the odd jobs that they did not have to do on the weekend. After this, I was called "Roni Toolbox," a loving term, I guess. I also encouraged each of them to know that all things are possible with God. He can do anything. If you really listen, He will teach you how to do them.

Perhaps you will try to do those little projects that you would like done. Try it, and talk to God for instruction. It is amazing what you can learn from Him. Remember, the Architect of the Universe was also a carpenter and engineer. Trust him with all your projects. He has the best way to do them, right at your fingertips.

$\mathcal{A}$ Most Magnificent Stove

*"But my God shall supply all your need according
to his riches in glory by Christ Jesus."*
—*Philippians 4:19*

In 1995 and 1996, it seems that most of the action occurred in my life shortly after I was called and anointed to teach. Some might say that this was a turbulent time, but I see it as a blessed time of many trials, but mighty miracles and blessings.

It was during this time that I decided to attend a countywide women's Bible study. It was held at one of the larger churches in the area, and more than a thousand women from the surrounding area attended. It was a very structured study with classes that ranged from eight to twelve people followed by a lecture-and-praise session. There was also homework to share in class the next week, and topped off with once-a-month luncheons at one of the team members' homes.

Having to be home most of the time with my husband, who was disabled, this outing was especially enjoyable for me. It also supplied me with other ladies to talk with, and to know more about the Word of God and how to share it with others. Another blessing to me was to be invited into other homes. I really enjoyed decorating, and to see the beautiful homes and how they were furnished was exciting to me. The ladies were always so gracious and willing to share their homes, and the luncheons were a real delight.

I knew that it would eventually be my turn to host the luncheon, and at that time my home was not the equivalent of the ones I had been in. I was almost embarrassed to have anyone in. My home had not been updated for many years, and with an invalid husband, I seldom had guests, and the house was not up to par for this. I immediately started to see if God would advise me regarding having my home prepared. Well, the story goes as follows.

After much prayer, I decided to ask my brother-in-law to assist me in updating my kitchen. He had been out of work for a short period of time, and before engaging in another job, I offered him the chance to do the kitchen with me. He agreed, and together we began to tear out the cabinets, countertops, and old appliances. We decided that the cabinets could be best and most economically done by replacing the doors and fronts of drawers, etc. So, that was our decision.

At that time, a local home-improvement store had the doors, drawers, and other things necessary to buy open stock. So, measurements were taken, and we were on our way. Finally, we had the supplies and proper sizes, and all we had to do was to match the paint for the existing shelves and install the doors and drawer fronts.

A few additional cabinets were added, and the new design was put into place. I had previously cut a hole in the wall to give access to the living room and dining area. Now, that wall would be replaced. We used the inside of the wall to create a pantry wall. This proved to be a very beautiful thing and added the pantry space I had lost.

A new stove and other appliances would be needed, so I began to shop around to get an idea of price and just exactly what I could buy to replace the old ones. I found they were very expensive, and I was beginning to get a bit discouraged in the search.

I went to several of the local appliance stores, and still no luck as to exactly what I wanted. So, I checked the mall. I went to the Sears store at Town Center, and there it was: exactly what I would like to have, but it cost too much. I had looked at other companies, and still the appliances were very expensive.

On that Saturday morning, I decided to go to an appliance outlet store. When I arrived, the lady named Betty came to assist me. I told her what I had seen at the mother store, and she said they did not have anything like that, as far as she knew. I told her that I had permission from the Lord to spend approximately six hundred dollars, so I wanted to stay in that range.

As I looked at all the other stoves, there just wasn't anything I really loved. She said that she did not know what was on the trailer in the back, but if I could come back on Sunday when they unloaded it, perhaps there was one on there. I explained that I taught a Sunday school class and could not come back on Sunday, so I would just have to accept one of the lesser ones.

As I continued to look, I came across a stove which was not nearly what I wanted, but I decided it was in the price range and it would be acceptable. I was trying to stay with that stove, because another couple was also looking at it, and I did not want them to buy it "out from under me," so I stayed with it. Betty, the salesperson, had disappeared from the floor, so I just waited by the stove I was choosing to buy.

Eventually, she came back to me and very strangely said, "Ma'am, I am trying to be discreet. Would you follow me please?"

Well, I did not know what she wanted. I wondered if they thought I was shoplifting or something. I just did not know. She advised me to please come with her to her supervisor. I followed through the offices. I knew I had not done anything wrong, but now I was back to the office of the supervisor.

When I arrived at the place where I was being taken, the lady, Betty, introduced me to her supervisor, who said, "Betty tells me that the Lord told her the stove you are supposed to have is on the trailer. I know Betty very well, and she would never ask me for such a favor unless she was certain that God told her this. We have looked on the trailer, and we have the stove she believes God wants you to have. I have given permission for it to be brought off."

They then took me to the back deck of the building, and there was the most magnificent stove, which had been $1,600 at the mother store. I said, "Yes, that is the stove I was looking at, but the price was too much."

The supervisor said, "This one is priced at six hundred dollars."

Betty looked at me and smiled. She said, "That is the price you told me God had allowed, right?"

I had to hold back the tears. I was thrilled beyond belief. You can bet I loaded that sucker up and took it home right then!

Well, when I arrived home, my daughter called me on my cell phone. She said she had been trying to reach me. She said, "The Lord told me you bought a stove, and I wanted to know where and how much." She said she had been praying that God would indeed lead me to what I wanted and not just what I needed. He did indeed, and now for the next miracle.

I wanted a microwave that would be an above-range microwave. One of the local discount stores had a sale on the over-the-range microwaves. I felt that the Lord would allow that price, and went into the store to purchase it. It was $399. When I got there, I was told that it was all sold out, so I looked at another one of lesser value, but they only had it in black.

The salesman said, "I am obligated to give you the next best, and after looking, the next best is our next to best."

So, I was able to purchase the matching microwave to the stove for the sale price. God was so good to me, and I was so thankful. It has now been twenty years, and both the microwave and stove are still working as they did the day I bought them. God provides us the best, never just the good, and He is the best of the best. He knew my need and indeed supplied it from His riches in glory.

I don't know about you, but this was pretty much a miracle for me, and I still praise my Lord for His generosity.

God Provided Our Home

"And into whatsoever house ye enter, first say, Peace be to this house."
—Luke 10:5

My husband and I had previously been given a lovely home, where we had lived for many years. It had been improved and redesigned to be just exactly what we wanted. We lived there until our children were grown, and this was indeed home, but now this home no longer served our needs. My husband's illness had brought him to a place where he was now bedridden. This was a split-level home, and stairs were just impossible to be able to get him in and out of the house. It was also a danger, because in event of a fire or storm, I would be unable to get him down the stairs. When there was any emergency that required him to go to the hospital, the fire department would have to be called to get him out. So, once again, we asked God for a home, one that would serve our needs.

We had considered building a home and having our daughter's family share this home, but God said, "This is not a good thing," and we were obedient. However, we did not give in until after the property on which to build was purchased. As with everything with God, He is able to turn even our mistakes into a blessing, and did so with this. Since it had been several years, the property value had doubled and brought a good profit when sold.

I had been invited to come to Ball Ground, Georgia, on this Saturday to watch my grandchildren parade for the beginning of baseball season. While up in this "neck of the woods," I also visited my older daughter, Kelli. She had, for a long time, wanted her dad and me to move closer to her, so this was the day she decided to help me find an appropriate house. I liked the style of her home very much, and was told that their builder had built this plan in a subdivision nearby. She insisted that we go and see those houses. While I was a little skeptical, I did go with her to some of the areas she suggested.

After driving by some of the subdivisions, I decided that these were not appropriate for us, because the lots were not level and therefore not easily accessible for my husband at this stage of his illness. Finally, she took me to another subdivision that was just being built. As we drove into the area, I quickly noticed a house which had a bay window, and I wanted to look at it.

Kelli insisted, "Mom, that is just a bunch of sticks. There is no way you can tell anything about that house."

I insisted, but she was adamant that we look at the homes she had brought me to see. We went on into the area to look at the houses that her builder had in construction process. Checking the lots and foundations carefully for possible handicap adjustments, we chose to look at two houses. We called the realtor, who was busy but asked that we wait for her here for thirty minutes. I told Kelli that while we waited for the realtor to show those houses, we could go back and look at the "sticks," just to bide our time.

We drove up to that house, got out, and went into the frame complex. There, we found a young man, who quickly warned us to be careful, because the posts that were in there were not attached and were temporarily holding up the beams of the ceiling. Interestingly enough, he told us that he was the builder, and began to describe what the house would look like when finished and how it could be made handicap-adapted. I knew without a doubt that God had chosen this house to be our home. At this point, the other homes in the subdivision were just not important to me, though I did go look at them.

My heart was full of excitement, and I could hardly wait to get home to tell Richard. I knew he would be excited, as well, and I also had to pray about it. I was unsure as to whether we could get the loan with my husband being so ill, and then to sell the house and the property . . .

My head was spinning. As I related to him all my concerns, he just pointed up. In other words, talk to God. I did do this, and decided to go online to see if we could qualify for a loan to purchase the house. When an agent called me back and I gave all our information, he checked everything out and called me back again. At this time, I remember how strange it was, because the man said, "I have been told to let you have anything you want." Today, I am wondering why I did not ask him who told him that, but then whoever did, God must have set it all up. I was immediately preapproved by phone, and the papers were en route to me to sign. Wow! I did not know it would be that easy.

So, I called the young builder and told him I had been preapproved, so would he please not allow anyone else to put in a bid until I could get back to him?

I decided to call the VA to see if they could be of help to us. Much to my surprise, they were not only able to help, but would give us a grant to handicap-adapt the home. This was the early week of March, and from that point on it rolled like wildfire.

First, a VA inspector—usually taking months, but with us it was days—then a VA loan was approved, and off we went to get the house completed quickly. Richard's condition was rapidly deteriorating, and his memory was very strained. God knew all this and was in control.

I remember the day the VA inspector came and gave instructions to the builders. After he left, I was talking to Brian and Sandy, the builders, and I asked them if they would join hands with me and pray about this. They agreed, and as I prayed, I noted that they were praying aloud, as well. When we finished, they both had tears in their eyes and hugged me. We all knew God was in charge. This was the first home they had built, and had prayed for a quick sale.

In the next days, more and more blessings and miracles came forth. God provided everything. As I prayed for countertops, he directed me to them. The same with tile, carpet, and—believe it or not—even the newly made window treatments at the old house fit right in. My God is an excellent decorator.

All was complete. Richard moved into the house on Father's Day. He was able to have his first shower in many years. The handicapped shower and all on one floor made it convenient to care for him better. I could roll him onto the screened porch in the morning for coffee, and roll him into the handicapped van to ride to see the wonderful views in the mountain area. What a home it was—close to my grandchildren and my girls, and easy care for Richard.

To everyone who entered this house, peace was met and praise for God was sure to be professed. We had indeed been given a miracle. My builders, being men of God, were excited to watch God work to bring everything about.

You see, Richard was deteriorating very rapidly. His memory was getting worse daily, and his ability to comprehend was even more depleted. He was unable now to even hold a pen to sign his name, and had to be coached to be able to do so. Time was of the essence. Richard had to be able to agree at the closing and be able to do so without question of his ability to understand. Only prayer could bring us through this portion of the miracle. The attorneys arrived at the house and took a video deposition to accompany our VA loan request. Praise God, Richard was able to do it.

It was finished. God had not only given us a new house, He supplied us the best of the best house—truly a home—truly a miracle.

$\mathcal{H}$e Is Going to Breathe

"The spirit of God hath made me, and the breath of the Almighty hath given me life."
—Job 33:4

I
n early October of 1995, my husband had been bedridden for quite a while. It had been suggested by physicians that because of his difficulty in swallowing that he have a feeding tube installed. This was not something I wanted to do to him. I felt that he had been deprived of most of the things that he enjoyed, and I did not want to take away one of the last things available for him. I would just be very cautious in what I fed him and to be with him when he would eat. I always cut his food in small pieces, as I had done for my children, and cautioned him as he ate to chew well.

He really wanted some steak one night, and I obliged him with this, being sure that it was cut into very small pieces and warning him to be especially careful. He enjoyed the meal and seemed to be fine afterward, and I had no idea of what had transpired—that being that he had aspirated, and a piece of the steak was lodged into his windpipe.

Days passed, and there was no indication of any problem, until he developed some fever and appeared to have some respiratory problems. He suffered for sleep apnea, and for that reason he slept with oxygen at all times. This night, the oxygen seemed to be of no effect for him, as he labored to breathe. When he showed evidence of stress and strangling somewhat, I called 911 to come to assist.

When the paramedics arrived, I gave them my assessment, which did not include any possibility that he had anything aspirated, because it had been three days and there had been nothing aspirated to my knowledge. When I followed the ambulance to the hospital emergency room and went to where he had been taken, much to my surprise, when he was "bagged" to help him breathe, out came a piece of steak from his windpipe area. Though it was no bigger than the tip of my finger, it had lodged in the windpipe and had caused irritation, and infection had set in. He was admitted to the hospital due to the fact that because of his multiple sclerosis of such a long existence, his immune system was very compromised. He was confined to the hospital for at least forty-eight hours to get ahold of the infection.

During this time, the doctor insisted that the feeding tube be put into place. It was just too dangerous for this to happen again. I agreed, and the procedure was done. Also at that time, the physician who was treating him, not being his regular doctor, was concerned that his blood pressure and other vitals were a bit unstable. He felt that there was something else going on, and suggested that a repeat MRI be done with contrast to see if there was something that had not been previously noted. Truly, this was the case: an egg-sized pituitary adenoma was discovered. This would grow with every bit of prolactin that the pituitary produced. The tumor had to be removed, or else it would continue to grow until it would invade every part of the brain.

We were ultimately referred to Emory University for consultation with a neurosurgeon for advice. After talking with the physician for some time, and with review of the MRI films, it was decided that surgery would be too dangerous. His brain had been very affected by the MS, and with that kind of damage already to his brain, anesthesia could render him a vegetable. There was, however, a new drug being tested that would gradually reduce the adenoma, if he was able to tolerate it. I prayed about this with Richard, and when the doctor came back into the room, we gave our decision to try the medication. With this decision, the physician, who was a professed Christian, agreed that the decision was the one he would choose if in the same situation. We received the prescription and went home to try and pray that he was able to tolerate.

He did fine on the medication, and we were told that this would take at least a year to reduce and that nothing would be noticed for at least three months. It was at this time, approximately Thanksgiving, and he was doing well with no complications due to the medication.

In February, once again he began to have problems: an exacerbation of the MS, as per usual, would show up again. His fever was extremely high, and I was unable to break the fever. Again, 911 was called and he was taken to the hospital. When his physician came in, he said he needed a cortisone injection to reduce the swelling to the brain. His brain stem was deeply scarred by the MS. Since the brain stem controlled the heart and lungs, and was life-threatening, fluids, antibiotics, and the steroidal medication was given IV.

Within ten minutes, he was comatose with temperature of 105 degrees and rising. They stabilized his pressure and rushed him to a room, where all monitors were placed and a watchful eye could be constantly on him. I checked him in and rushed up to the room, only to find that the nurses were turning off the monitors. They informed me, "He is gone, Mrs. Zubiena. I am so sorry."

I was in shock and insisted, "No, he is not dead! He is going to breathe. You don't understand. He does this sometimes, but he will breathe." They rushed to call the chaplain and to notify my daughter who worked in the admissions office. I insisted, "Keep the oxygen on, because he will breathe."

With that, the nursing supervisor did put the oxygen back on, but added, "We always check to make sure. You see, what we do is to take a tissue and fold it into a point, then we touch the pupil of the eye. If there is no reflex, then we know the patient is gone. Now, watch closely. I am touching the pupil. See, there is no reflex. The heart monitor is flatlined. The brain monitor is flatlined. There is no blood pressure and no respiration. You see, Mrs. Zubiena, he had a respiratory arrest and subsequent cardiac arrest. He is gone, honey. I am sorry, but he is gone."

I immediately rebuked this and I insisted, "He is going to breathe."

With that, a young nurse standing by me asked, "Would you like me to pray with you?"

I replied, "Yes, please do." The nurse placed one hand on my husband's wrist and the other on mine, and started to pray for peace and contentment and for God's grace and mercy. After several sentences, she stopped and exclaimed, "I feel a pulse!"

The nursing supervisor immediately stated that it was just reflex and not to be concerned.

The nurse began to pray again, and once again she stopped and said, "Mrs. Ellis, I am definitely getting a pulse. It is weak, but there is definitely a pulse."

At this point, all monitors were turned back on and the blood pressure was pumped up again. Now there was a pressure of very low grade, but some pressure. They began to listen for heart and respiration. Nothing there.

My daughter who had arrived said to me, "Mama, tell him to breathe. He will listen to you."

With that, I leaned over into his face and, as if I were forcing the air into him, I said, "Breathe, Richard. Breathe."

Suddenly, he gasped and began to breathe. All monitors were once again responding. His heart rate was weak, but normal. Blood pressure, normal; pulse, normal; and respiration, normal.

During the time that we were dealing with the above account, the doctors had been notified of his "death," and the funeral home called to come for the body. As our primary physician came in, the supervisor said, "He is back."

With that, Dr. Fortson, for whom I had worked when he first set up his office, exclaimed, "I am not surprised! I know this girl." He advised, "Roni, I do not believe he will wake up, though. I think there is too much damage to his brain, and with the thirteen minutes he was without oxygen to his brain, if by some chance he does wake, he will go again, and will be pretty much unresponsive." He hugged me and said, "Call me. Whatever time it is, I will be here with you."

Shortly thereafter, my younger daughter and son came in and were upset, to say the least. My younger daughter went over to her daddy, and with tears and begging, she asked, "Daddy, would you please not leave me? You have to be here to give me away at my wedding."

While she was begging her dad, my other daughter noticed, "Mom, he hears her. Look, he is moving his toes." Indeed, he was responding, and with that, once again, my daughter said, "Mom, tell him to open his eyes."

The chaplain tried to dissuade us, stating he may be frightened because he cannot open his eyes. With that, my daughter said, "No, my dad trusts my mother, and he will do what she tells him. Tell him, Mom, to open his eyes."

Once again, I leaned over into his face and said, "Honey, try to open your eyes. If you can't yet, that is okay, but try."

With that, he began to blink terribly rolled back eyes, and eventually the eyes came to center, and he opened them and looked around. He said, "What are all y'all doing here?"

My son said, "You've been gone a while. Welcome back."

Immediately, my daughter ran to his side and began to ask if he could remember seeing Jesus or what he may have seen. But, at that point the neurologist came in and interrupted. After a few neurological questions, he stated how amazing this was, and what a miracle.

Shortly after the doctor left, my son asked if there was anything he wanted or would like to have. My husband answered, "Yes, a hamburger and a cup of coffee."

We all laughed and were so thankful. All through the rest of the day and that night and the next few days, multiple hospital personnel and doctors came by to see the man who had miraculously come back to life. Within a week, he was able to come home and was doing well.

God had performed a real miracle that day for many to see, but the miracle was just half done. The following week, as I sat on my porch questioning my God, "Why, with his condition, did you kill him and then bring him back? Why?" I cried out to my God, "Why?"

With a real shocking reply, my God answered, "The tumor is gone."

I said, "What?"

God once again said, "The tumor is gone. Deprivation of oxygen suffocated the tumor. Get confirmation."

I immediately ran to the phone and called Emory Clinic to the neurosurgeon, and told them what had happened and what God had said to me. I was told to bring my husband in the following day for a repeat MRI with contrast to get confirmation.

When I arrived at the clinic, though everyone was nice to me, I felt that they were just pacifying me and truly did not believe me. They did the MRI and sent us home to await the results. About 4:30 p.m., the phone call came. The physician's assistant asked me to hold for the doctor. The doctor came on the line and stated that he had a conference call set up with the radiologist, and that the radiologist would give me the report. He stated, "Well, Mrs. Zubiena, by comparison to the previous film and the one done today, there is no other way to say it except the tumor is indeed gone. We have indeed witnessed a miracle!"

God had really attested to His majesty and power. We tell everyone we can, but not only did we tell it, but all those skeptics who were just really nice to us. What a witness! What a mighty God! How blessed we were to have been given such mercy and miracle.

Miracle of Sight

"And as Jesus passed by, he saw a man who was blind from his birth. . . . When he had
thus spoken, he spat upon the ground, and made clay of the spittle, and He anointed the
eyes of the blind man with the clay, and said unto him, Go, wash in the pool of Siloam.
[The man] went his way therefore, and washed, and came seeing."
—*John 9:1, 6–7*

A s I read this scripture, I was so intrigued that this man was given such a gift. I was excited to just imagine how he must have felt. He, never before having had the gift of the miracle of sight, what possibly could have been going through his mind when first he was able to see? I remembered how clearly I once could see, and how my vision now at this age had somewhat diminished. If only I could see as well as when I was younger.

I was reminded of a time when I was just a youngster and would visit my granny's house, and I remembered her terribly thick glasses. It was almost frightful to look her straight in the face, because her eyes, through those glasses, were very large and scary. They were so very thick and framed with wire rims that sat tightly on her nose. Granny was a tall, slim woman with salt-and-pepper gray hair, and those very blue eyes would magnify and look nearly through you. She was a humble woman and loved her Jesus with all her heart. I never heard her raise her voice, but she certainly could speak with authority and gaze over the glasses to such extent that I knew not to cross her at all. She was also a woman of few words, but when she spoke, there was a kind of wisdom that flowed from her that you would know she was blessed.

Every morning, my granny could be found in her room before anything else, reading her Bible. She said, "The first fruit of the day belongs to the Lord." I would see her sitting there with her Bible on her lap and a ribbon there to hold her place so that she would know where to start again the next day. When Granny closed that book, you did not dare to speak to her, because now was her time talking and listening to the Lord. This was a great influence to me as I grew into adulthood.

Always, though, the glasses were right there on her nose. Never did I see her without them. You can just know how I felt when I came in one day and Granny was not wearing her glasses. She looked a bit strange, but when I asked about her glasses, she spoke not a word, but my Aunt Edith replied, "Mama does not need her glasses anymore. She has received second sight."

I had not heard that expression before, and so I did not understand what was being told to me, but essentially, God had rewarded my Granny's obedience by restoring her sight to perfect. She could read her Bible without glasses, and even thread a needle without glasses. Aunt Edith was really excited about this miracle of sight for her mother, but my granny never boasted, only said, "God is so good." God had indeed given my granny a gift, and she never again wore those old wire-rimmed glasses—or any other glasses—as long as she lived.

As I recalled this story of my granny, I reflected on some other miracles that I was attempting to write down. I noticed that my vision was becoming increasingly poor. A friend shared that he was having cataract surgery, and I inquired about it and followed up with the surgeon he had recommended. I found that I, too, had cataracts, and made arrangements to have this corrected.

Understand that God healed my granny's vision, and I know He certainly could heal mine, but I also know that He had given the gift of healing to some wonderful doctors who can do miraculous things now that were not available when Granny was in need. So, I made the appointment with Dr. Mitchell. Now I, too, was on my way to a renewed vision.

I knew a little bit about blindness from an incident I suffered in the late 1950s. I had been somewhat restless and was looking for more excitement in my life, and when my sister and brother-in-law saw an ad in the paper for dance instructor, that seemed to be it. This was a training class to go to work teaching dancing for Arthur Murray Studios. We all liked to dance and thought this would be a fun thing. Joe and I had worked part time in high school assisting with a local dance studio, and so we were somewhat aware of what to do. Little did we know how extensive the training would be and what would be required of us.

After filling out the application, we were there for the first training session. There was a large group who had come to learn to dance, and that was the purpose of some. We wanted that, too, but thought we might pursue the employ if it paid well. Each night of training, one after the other was eliminated. Now it was down to a class of approximately twenty people, still to be further eliminated.

Joe had a job at Lockheed Aircraft, and Joyce and I were working at the hospital, so we did not really need the work, but it was fun. After a while, Joyce decided not to do this, and it would interfere with Joe's work, so they dropped out. I stayed on and graduated the class and became an instructor. It was hard work, and being on your feet for hours with high heels was sometimes painful, but I stayed with it. It was during this time that I suffered blindness.

As many of you may have seen movies where there was a grand ballroom and the dancers were swirling around the floor in a grand waltz, those dancers were professional dancers. This was called on by Hollywood to have inserts done to dub into movies. We were called on to perform one of these movie dubs. It was held at the Georgian Terrace Hotel on Ponce de Leon Avenue in Atlanta, Georgia. This was an old, grand hotel with a magnificent ballroom. It had inlaid marble throughout and beautiful crystal chandeliers, magnificent architectural features, and a wonderful dance floor. The Hollywood company furnished the costumes and we went for our fittings and hairdos, etc.

It was the day of "shooting," so to speak. We had to be there early for makeup application and final fitting of costumes. Many huge lights were set up, and their intensity was almost blinding. Makeup was another thing; it was extremely heavy, and especially the eye makeup, to make us look good on camera. Once, twice, and finally the third shoot, and it was a "wrap." We were all going to be in the movies.

After finish, we removed the costumes and placed them back in the proper containers and went to remove the false eyelashes and thick makeup. All over and with tired feet, I went home. It was not long before I felt the itch of my eyes. It was so intense, I could hardly stand it. I kept putting cold compresses on them, but nothing helped. It was then that I saw a bottle of bacteria medication to cleanse cuts and scrapes, etc. The label clearly gave a warning: *Do not get into eyes, could do dangerous damage.* Well, I was not going to get it in my eyes. I was just going to dab it on the lids to stop the itching. With the extreme irritation, it burned and my eyes watered, and you guessed it: now it was in my eyes. I washed it with cold water immediately, but the damage had occurred.

The following morning, when I got up to prepare for work, my eyes were very blurred and my vision was limited. I could not catch the trolley to work; I had to call a taxi. When I got to work, everyone there was concerned with the swollen and red eyes, and insisted that I see a doctor. One of the office personnel called her ophthalmologist and made me an emergency appointment. I called a taxi, but when I arrived at the Georgia Baptist Medical building, I could not see to go in. I could not see to pay the taxi, and I was in a lot of pain. The taxi driver was a kind and trustworthy man. He helped me into the building and would not take any money from me. He asked a lady who was waiting for the elevator to help me get to the physician's office, which she graciously accommodated me.

After the examination, and the bad news that I had burned holes in my corneas, I asked about returning to work; I had students waiting. The doctor informed me that he was going to have to patch the worst eye with both gauze and a black patch, and the other he would leave for me to apply the patch when I arrived home. He said, "I cannot tell you until you return in three days if your trauma is going to permanently blind you."

I was really scared. I had done a stupid thing, and I was paying a terrible price. He gave me some samples of drops and a sample of pain medication, and they walked me down to get into a taxi for home. The previous cab driver had given me his cab number and told me to call him if I needed help. He came to pick me up and helped me into my apartment. I thanked him, and he left.

I was alone in an apartment without anyone to take care of me, not even a telephone. I was scared, in pain, and could only see gray clouds. People were just shadows. I laid down and wanted to cry, but crying would be all the worse for this injury, so I tried to keep calm. The pain medication made me drowsy, and I went to sleep. After a couple of hours, I was awakened by my boyfriend that I only knew by his voice; I could not see him at all. After that, everyone was made aware of my situation, and many came by to check on me and offer to bring me food, etc.

It is of note to mention I did not know how much eyes were a factor in the rest of body functions. I found that I could not eat with a fork; I could not find my mouth. Also, it seemed that my nose ran constantly and that I developed a type of urinary problem; I had to go constantly. I knocked things over, and although you think you know your house, when you are blind your depth perception and space is unsure. You run into things, and there is danger of falling, stumbling, and all those possibilities. I had really done a piece of work on myself. Not only had I done damage to my eyes, I also was not paid if I did not work.

Three days passed, and I went back to the doctor with wonderful news. The damage was healing well, and I was able to remove the patch from my left eye. I was able to return to work and teach with a black patch on, but my students had been made aware of my condition, so they were most compassionate to me.

After another week, the other patch was off, and my eyes were healing well and went on to complete recovery. I was thankful that I was okay, and learned to respect the labels that the medications place on them are to be followed.

As I remembered this, I once again pondered the surgery I was about to receive. I prayed, and my God assured me that all would be okay. My church, friends, and family were praying, too, so I was now ready to go forth with my upcoming surgery.

On April 7, 2010, I was to begin my drops in the right eye, which would prepare it for surgery on the following day. I was really excited to get this done since the good report that my friend Dana had. So, I ate a nice dinner and nothing to eat or drink after midnight, as ordered, and watched my TV shows. I fully expected to not be able to watch TV the following day, post-surgery.

I awakened early at 6:00 a.m., as per usual, and had my Bible reading, "daily bread," and time with the Lord. I prayed for His protection and for His blessings upon the physician who was to do the surgery. I also prayed for my friend Dana, who was to have his second eye done today. All preparation was complete, and I awaited my daughter to come for me. Kelli would drive me there and stay there with me until surgery was complete.

Shortly after arriving and checking in, Dana and his son, Will, would arrive and check in just after me. I really hated to allow them to see me, because really I knew that without makeup, I was not a good specimen. I swallowed my pride and went over to them. Shortly thereafter, an announcement was made that there would be a two to three hour delay. We could either wait or reschedule for another day. I was all prepared, both mentally and physically, so I elected to wait, as did Dana. So, we all watched a news report, and read magazines, and visited occasionally.

Finally, the time was come, and they called my name—of course, not correctly, but I told them the correct pronunciation and got up to follow back to the surgery-preparation area. As I walked out, Dana called to me and motioned that he and Will would be praying. I signaled a thumbs up and went on in.

When I got into the prep area, I was surprised that it looked just like a dental office with a similar chair. They questioned as to my name and my birthdate, and asked which eye I was to have worked on today. I told them the right one, and they verified that there was a mark above that right eye to ensure that the surgeon would operate on the appropriate one.

Then, the IV. Usually I have no problem with them hitting my vein, but wouldn't you know, this would be the day. Well, I told them just wait a moment, and I would have the Lord prepare the next place. They obliged me, and indeed as I asked, the vein was easily "hit and threaded." Now the IV was in place, and next came the numbing drops for the eye. They warned that these would burn a little, but it was far less than getting a little soap in your eyes.

About that time, Dana was brought in and put in a chair two stalls away, and I heard him answering all the questions that I had been asked and given the same instructions. The anesthetist was here, again confirming my name and birth, and which eye was to be worked on today. Then she stated that she was going to give me an injection in the IV, and this would make me relax. I would not go to sleep, though.

They called and were ready for me in OR, and the medication was started. They lowered the chair into stretcher position and placed a pillow under my head, and started to roll me to the door. I saw Dana and said, "Dana, I am going in now." I knew that he would immediately pray for me, and I was completely at ease with everything.

I remember seeing the door open to take me into the operating room, but I never saw the other side of the door, nor did I see the operating room. The next thing I heard was the nurse and my daughter saying, "We need to get you into the wheelchair. You are ready to go home." Wow, I could hardly believe it was over! It seemed that I had only just gone in, and now I was ready to leave. I had no pain, no remembrance of anything going on, and I was ready to go home.

Well, Kelli brought the car to the exit, and they helped me into it. I could see just as well as I had before the operation, but much brighter. I got into the car and told Kelli, "I am hungry."

She said, "Me, too." So, we went to the local restaurants and had a full meal. Can you believe that? Immediately after I awoke from the anesthesia, I was not only able to see without problems, but was steady enough and ready to eat in a restaurant. How amazing was that? Praise God for His care of me.

The rest of the time was pretty funny. I came home and put the drops in my eyes, and decided to take a short nap. About an hour later, I got up and noted that the rain had stopped and the sun was shining through the front window. As I walked into the kitchen, my white countertops, which I thought were dingy, were suddenly vibrantly white to the extent I had to grab the extremely dark glasses that were provided for me to wear. From that point on, the miracle of sight was explosive. The tulips that I thought were pink were a beautiful lavender, and sky was so blue, I was dazzled. All the colors were so vivid, I could hardly remember what they had been before, only they were so beautiful, I was spellbound.

On Sunday morning, I went to church, and as I was driving down Hwy 53, just as I topped the hill, a panoramic view of the mountains came into my sight. I suddenly saw that those beautiful mountains, were covered with individual trees, all different shades of green and textures of pine and oak, and then the redbuds in the mix. I was sure that the people behind me wanted that "drunk" off the road. I was indeed drunk with God's glorious creations. I just wanted to look and look. It was as if I was seeing this for the first time. I praised God and thanked Him all the way there.

When I got to the Sunday school class, everyone was coming over to see how I was, and then came Dana with no glasses on, and how excited we both were with our new vision. Jokingly, Charles, my pastor, made a quick joke to the class and stated that I did not know until now that he was a white man. We all laughed, and I told them that I also thought that I was tall, but now the floor was closer so I realized that I am but a short shrimp. Not to mention that I also had to look in the mirror, and realized I would need a really good steam iron or a good plastic surgeon. My wrinkles made the skin on my face appear to not fit, like it belonged to someone else. Well such for the jokes, the surgery was successful and miraculous. I thank my God for the wonderful gift He had given me in a surgeon to which He had provided such expertise.

The second surgery was one week later, and once again, I was very calm. I did see a lot of what was going on at this time, but it seemed everything happened so fast and it was over. Again, no pain, no irritation, and no residual of anesthesia. This lens was the reading lens. The first was for far vision, and this one for intermediate vision and reading. It is amazing what can and is being done to improve vision now.

I came home and I could read a telephone book without my glasses. I could read my Bible without lifting the glasses to look out the bottom. I also am right now typing on my computer, and all is clear as can be.

Would you say that I am happy about this? You bet I am. I had no idea my vision was so bad. I had been on a trip to Florida with a friend who had asked me to look for a particular sign, and I was not able to see it. That was my first knowledge of deteriorating of my vision. I certainly did not wait, but went straight to have this corrected. I don't have to constantly look for the glasses I was always misplacing, nor will I have to worry about them breaking again and not being able to afford to replace them.

My granny had second sight. My God, through a talented, gifted surgeon, has given me second sight. I praise Him and glorify Him for all the blessings, especially for the miracle of sight.

Lord, My Car's in My Garden

"Who is like unto thee, O Lord, among the gods? Who is like thee, glorious in holiness, fearful in praises, doing wonders?"
—*Exodus 15:11*

Freak accident or divine lesson, I really feel both in this situation. Sometimes I am like Martha, sister of Lazarus: I am always in a tizzy and somewhat scattered. In these times, I really don't react as an intelligent species of womanhood. I just act, often to my sincere regret. I will say things off the top of my head, jump into a situation without thinking it out, and most always regret my actions and words. God says to listen to Him and He will guide us in the path of righteousness, also in the way we should go. I should have listened, but as per usual, I pass it off. I am too smart to make that mistake, or not me, God. Well . . .

On several occasions I have left the house, and then when in my car, out of the garage, and in the driveway, I remember something I needed to take with me. I put the car into park, mash the garage-door opener, and leave the car running while I run into the house to retrieve what I left behind. Once, I nearly got out of the car when I realized I had not placed the gear in park, and immediately put it in park and ran into the house. That was a warning. Then several days earlier, I left the house again and forgot something. I did the same thing, and even got in the car and realized I had also forgotten something else, and did it again. Another warning.

Every day, my grandchildren came to my house on the bus to await their mother coming home from work. I leave the garage door open for them to come in, and that is almost always the end of it. Today, I needed to run some errands, so I offered to take them to get ice cream on the way. This we did, to their happiness, and upon returning home, I had my hands full of dry cleaning and mistakenly left the keys in the car. So, when I was ready to leave for my Bible study, I was stressed, because I could not find my keys. I looked everywhere and was very frustrated, bringing on my first mistake. I asked my granddaughter to check the car to see if I had left them there.

Suddenly, I heard the car start up. I ran to the garage door leading out to the car and sure enough, my keys were in the car, and she had taken the liberty to start the car up. I really fussed at her and gave her a lecture on what could happen if the car had been in gear. I told her, "You could have gone through the wall and into the yard, and been seriously injured." I admonished her to never do that again.

After that, I got my Bible, my book that was being studied, and made sure I had paper and pen for notes. I went out and got into the car. I backed the car out, and once again I had forgotten something. The sun was very bright this afternoon, and having just previously completed cataract surgery, sunglasses are a must.

I had already pushed the remote in the car to close the garage door. I stopped the car, placed it in drive, and came forward to the door, and pushed the remote again, opening the garage door. Since I was in a hurry, I did not wait for the door to be fully open; I just got out of the car. I noticed three young teens walking down the street and waved to them, and when I turned back around, the car was moving forward into the garage. I tried quickly to get into the car, but failed, and started to hang onto the steering wheel to pull myself in. I did not think I had time to get in, so I reached my right leg in to hit the brake. I missed the brake, but very efficiently engaged the gas pedal. Holding on to the steering wheel, and off balance with the left leg, I was being dragged and could not take my foot off. It was like you saw in the movie, where the young man played hooky from school and his friend and he ran the sports car through the garage.

I was thoroughly shocked. It happened so fast, I could not respond. The car crashed through the wall to the outside. Fortunately, the car hit a very strong corner post and bounced off, but caused the right-front wheel to totally collapse. I was sitting behind the wheel and put on the emergency brake. Had that wheel not collapsed, I don't know what the outcome could have been—certainly much worse. I put the car in park, turned the engine off, and wondered how this could be.

The three young teens came running, fully expecting me to be seriously injured, if not dead. I opened the car door and got out on my own. By then, neighbors were running to see about me, and I was completely dumbfounded as to what to do now. In shock for sure, so terribly concerned that my azaleas were going to be ruined. Funny, my house was a pile of debris and my car probably totaled, and I was concerned about my azaleas and hostas. Now you know why they call me "Rhododendron Zucchini."

I am so blessed to be alive and not seriously injured. Certainly, the angels were indeed watching over me, and I am blessed by my Daddy who always takes care of me. I want you to know that I had prayed an unusual prayer from the swing that morning. As I got up to come into the house, I said, "Lord, dispatch angels to watch over me today. I am such a fuddy duddy."

I truly believe He turned to His angels and gave the order, "She is not kidding, so get on your way. She is going to need you." Indeed, I was protected. How I got into the car before crashing through the wall, I don't know, and then my left leg was on the ground, and just a bruise on my ribs from falling against the seatbelt holder. How is it possible I am okay?

Of interest, there were things I wanted to do to the garage anyhow, and now these could be done at no expense to me. Also, I can clear out the "junk" that someone could be using instead of me hoarding. God knows me so well and always finds a way to do just the thing that will benefit me. Again, this was an accident of my doing, because I did not listen to my God's warning, but He is faithful and is always there when I need Him. He has assured me in Matthew 10:31, "Do not fear therefore; you are of more value that many sparrows."

As God reminded me of what value I represent to Him, I began to share this blessing and miracle with my "adopted" son, Bruce. Bruce had done many construction jobs for me before, and I was always pleased with the work. We had become very close. Bruce's mom lived out in the Midwest, and he did not get to see her very often, so I became a substitute.

As soon as I had time to think after this happened, I called Bruce and told him I needed him. He says, "You about scared me to death. I could hear it in your voice, this was serious." Well, it was serious, and I did not know if the roof was about to fall in or not, so Bruce could certainly tell me and secure the area. Indeed, Bruce came with his wife, Becky, and just took over for me. He is a very intelligent man and so is his wife, so they were a great source of information for me.

Bruce efficiently measured and assessed the situation. He then went to the local home-improvement store and purchased his immediate needs to "shore up" the area. Becky began to pick up debris and clean up. I was on the phone constantly with friends who had heard about the mishap and wanted to inquire about my condition. I also was talking with the insurance company and potential adjusters to get permission to remove the car. When we had permission, a wrecker was called to come and evaluate.

Bruce was able to remove the broken studs and put in temporary ones to hold things together for the night. He then called the wrecker company and told them to wait until the next morning so that daylight could give more direction. It was going to be a difficult job where it was located. This was a somewhat enclosed area, and there were other garden areas that I did not wish to have destroyed. Of course, also the garage door was torn off, and that could not be shut either. It was dusk and little light, so we decided to call it a night.

Bruce and Becky were here early the next morning, and clean-up was foremost at the time. Andy's wife called and said he was on the way with the equipment to get the car out. I asked the children to help remove my hostas, and there was a clear area to remove the car. Andy and Bruce assessed the situation to be best handled with a Bobcat, so the Bobcat people were called and came right away. You have to really give credit where credit is due: it was simply amazing how they were able to turn the car and pull it out with little damage to my sidewalks or lawn. It took less than ten minutes, and the car was loaded up and headed to the repair shop.

Now, back to the work at hand. Bruce and Becky loaded up the rest of the torn-up wall.

Later that afternoon, the garage-door man came and began to remove the old, torn-up door and make ready to replace it with a beautiful sunrise-design door. This was Bruce's suggestion to have it correspond with the arches on the front of the house. As we talked about this and about some beautifully colored bruises I now was sporting, I again spoke of my gratefulness to God and the miracle we had just experienced.

With that, Bruce said, "The blessing and miracle went wider than that, Roni," and he turned to Becky and said, "Tell her what happened."

Becky related, "Bruce had been in Huntsville, Alabama, and had just come in when you called. Also, he was scheduled to do a job in Dublin, Georgia, which was just postponed for a few days. We also were in need of that job for our own survival, so—"

Bruce broke in with, "God had a much wider need than you knew, but God knew." Bruce was not only available to do the work, but was in need of the work. God was there for all of us. Then there was the shadow effect: my grandchildren were not in the garage or prayer garden when this happened. They saw how dangerous playing around with a car can be, and the lesson for me and anyone else who might read this account. There is no greater God than He.

The house was quickly being repaired with a window installed. The new garage door is a thing of beauty. I am okay, and all is well with my soul. Thanks be to my wonderful Architect, Engineer, and Designer, not to mention Protector, Provider, and my Comforter. Praise His name. Prayer changes things, changes the whole scenario, and only through prayer could all this have been accomplished.

The adjuster says my beautiful fountain will be replaced, as will the bench and other things in my garden, and prayer can begin there again. I hope you will be blessed by this account and take heed to the warning. Do not exit your car while the engine is running, and double-check the gear and brake.

It was indeed a miracle, and I claim it to you today.

The Pink Mountain

"But as it is written, Eye hath not seen, nor ear heard, neither have entered into the heart of man, the things which God hath prepared for them that love him."
—*1 Corinthians 2:9*

How blessed I have been all my life! Even in the bad circumstances, God has always come through for me in mighty ways. Most recently, it seems, just since I have become a widow, God has brought forth so many wonderful gifts to me, I can hardly believe it. Very special things that I know are just for me, so I really want others to know how loving and wonderful He is. God is no respecter of persons, and what He does for me He will surely do for you. Just look for His wonderful blessings that He gives so freely. I love Him so much, just for who He is, and then to have the extra blessing of gifts is just more than I could ever begin to dream.

Early last fall, I was recovering from eye surgery. I marveled at the things I could see. The mountains took on an all-new excitement with the numerous colors and textures. This morning, the scene once again illuminated. As I sat in my swing praising the Lord for all the many blessings He has afforded me, my eyes were suddenly drawn to the distant mountain ridge that is readily visible from here at the top of my yard.

As I praised the Lord for good vision and related the beautiful sight I was seeing, there it was: suddenly, without any gradual appearance at all, the mountain peak turned a vibrant pink and appeared to be radiating, as if uplifting arms to the heavens. The range of trees beside it were still displaying the amazing colors of autumn, but the mountain peak was saturated in this lustrous, bright pink. I was so moved with gratitude that I began to cry and thank God for such a beautiful sight.

In total joy, I jumped up and ran into the house. I quickly grabbed my camera and rushed back out to capture the wondrous sight. As I stood there clicking, taking pictures from all angles, I was excited to share my precious gift with all I could. Then, a disappointed letdown when I was set to view the photos I had taken and just given thanks to God for the gift. In shock, I noticed the pictures reflected only the mountain view; the majestic color was not there at all. It was just as any other day with the mountain view.

"Why, Lord? Why did the pictures not reflect your precious gift, as I had seen?" I asked. I so wanted to show them to everyone.

I felt the Lord was saying to me, "They were just for you, Revonda, no one else."

You know, I am just a plain person, no celebrity, no royalty, of no specific importance at all, yet my God gave me a pink mountain. I remembered about Jackie Kennedy Onassis being married to one of the wealthiest men in the world, who gave her all sorts of gifts, but even at that, he could not give her a pink mountain, but the Lover of my Soul gave me such a wondrous gift. So undeserving am I, but still He gifted me. How very special He makes me feel to know that He, the King of Kings and Lord of Lords, loves me.

Again, I remind you that He is no respecter of persons and has wondrous gifts with which to dazzle us, if only we trust Him and praise Him. Indeed, "ear hath not heard nor eye seen the wondrous gifts He has in store for those who love and trust Him." If He gives such wonderful gifts to us, how much more fulfilled we will be to give to those whom we love.

$\mathcal{R}$ed Light, Green Light

"Hope deferred maketh the heart sick: but when the desire cometh, it is a tree of life."
—Proverbs 13:12

D o you ever have times when even though you know what God would say about a situation, you just can't turn loose and let Him take it? I sometimes feel that God must be really disappointed in me. With all the miracles He has provided me, I still question and complain, and just fail to allow Him to be in charge. I know full well that when He is in charge, "all things work together for good to them that love God" (Romans 8:28).

I had suffered through a broken relationship, in which God had really taken care of me. Part of that care was my grandson Cory, who stood by me through it all. He would just come by to check on me and talk to me about the Lord, call for lunch, and even be my date to plays, etc. Indeed, Cory was a blessing, and God was even more real when Cory was around me. This is the same grandson miracle I have written about in the story "Pride and Joy."

I had to be put to the test. Was I going to allow God to be the one in whom I put my trust, or am I trusting in another? This was played out in an unusual and miraculous way when Cory applied for a job. He had previously served his internship for his master's degree with a very prominent world charity organization in Washington State. Cory had never forgotten how really wonderful the people were there, and hoped he would get the opportunity to serve God with them. Nonprofit ministry was his heartstring, and he sincerely wanted to serve with this charity.

Sometime in the early part of July, a position became available with the very charity he so desired to join. He applied for the job and waited. In the interim, he had a friend who worked with a state university who made him aware of a really excellent position available there. Not knowing what was ahead with any of the applications he had submitted, Cory applied for this position, as well. Weeks passed, and no news from any of his applications. I was praying, my prayer partners were praying, and Cory was fasting and praying for an answer.

Understand that when Cory applied for all these positions, I was behind him 100 percent in whatever he wanted to do . . . right? I thought I was, until he received an answer from the charity for whom he so wanted to work. He was offered an entry position with a reasonable salary, but mostly it was doing the Lord's work with the company and people he cared about. How great was that? Well, exciting for Cory, not so for me. That would mean that my Cory would be on the other side of the country from me.

I suddenly became ill. I literally was nauseated to think that I would no longer have Cory with me. I didn't tell him about this, but I sincerely allowed myself some time to pray. I called on good Christian friends, who seemed surprised that I, of all people, would feel this way. My guilt was overwhelming. I felt that with all my miracles that God had provided, and now I am crying because I would not have Cory with me.

God knew my pain. Perhaps he was a little disappointed in me, but nevertheless, He never left me. I could feel a comradeship with some of my church family who had sent their sons and daughters off to war and who were serving in the mission field far away. The support I received was wonderful. Many prayers went up on my behalf and on Cory's, as well. People who knew him and knew his desire to serve were excited for him.

As I was about to be reconciled with this devastating event in my life, up popped a most unusual situation. Suddenly, he was given the opportunity to work for the state university, as well. My faith was stretched even further, not to mention how Cory's was being stretched. Certainly, I was happy that he might not go away at all if he were to decide to take this job instead. Well, you know where I stood with this one, not to mention that it would pay him some $11,000 more per year. I would not have to get on an airplane to see him, and I could call him at will—all the things I so wanted would still be in place. All I had to do was to convince him to take this job.

Enter Satan. "Just convince him. Anyhow, it was more money. He would not have to move across country. He is young and can always do that charity work later." You see where this was going. My test was to leave it alone, not to touch it in any direction.

As prayers flooded in for both of us, I was given a clear view of my place here, and God was adamant. I did indeed release it to Him and pulled back. Now it was in God's hands, and Cory would now be put to the test, his desire to work for the charity against working in a secular position.

Some may say that it would be God's will for him to work for the nonprofit ministry, but my very wise pastor suggested a different scenario. What if God intended Cory to be a light in a dark corner? Perhaps God would choose to use him in the secular job to lead someone to Christ? So, Pastor Charles prayed, "Lord, I am going to ask you to give Cory discernment and further that you, Lord, will give a definite green light to one and a very clear red light to the other." This prayer was prayed during intercessory prayer and was in agreement with five people. God has said that when two or more are in one accord, He is in the middle.

Cory was told by both interviewers that an answer had to be there by Friday of the same week. Cory prayed, as did others, and then a friend said, "Perhaps you should consult the *Book of Proverbs*. When I am in a dilemma, it always helps me."

Cory responded by doing just that. He turned to Proverbs and received the Word to listen to his elders and ultimately to God. Cory called me for lunch on Thursday and handed me a paper. I had suggested that he write down the good about each and bad about each and compare. When it came to the bottom line, they were about the same all the way. Still, no decision.

Thursday night we talked again, and he said, "Meemaw, I am just twenty-four years old. I have no wife, no house payment, no car payment, and I have a savings account to last me more than a month. Money is just not a factor in this." I agreed with him that what had to take priority was what God would choose him to do.

After a sleepless night, and realizing that what Cory was saying was "I am probably going to be going to Washington," I felt peace in my heart. It was okay with me, and I told God so. I did indeed have peace about it, and felt assured that I would find some way to see my grandson, and all would be well. Cory, on the other hand, was still struggling. I prayed for him peace in whatever he chose.

Later, during one of my sleepless times, I went in to my computer to check my emails and found many assurances. I also found another amazing development: the gentleman with whom I had the broken relationship was asking me to have lunch with him on Friday. I agreed, and thanked God for some kind of renewed friendship to occur.

As I arose the next morning, I went to my private place to be with the Lord. This was at the top of my yard on an outdoor swing. As I talked to God and voiced my despair at the thought of once again being alone, quite a strange phenomenon occurred. As I looked out in the distance to the mountains, fog was moving in. Little by little, it covered the mountains, then the trees, and slowly moved toward my subdivision. I sat there in amazement, and the mist covered all the surrounding houses, trees, and eventually then to my trees, and my house, and me. It was almost scary. Suddenly, there was nothing but me and the swing on which I was sitting. I was aware that there were no birds singing, no sound of traffic on the near highway, just silence and the surrounding fog-mist that encompassed me. I felt that the Lord was saying to me, "Alone? *This* is alone. *Nothingness* is alone, but you are not alone, for even now, I am with you and will never leave you."

I took a deep breath and agreed with my God, and I gave it all to Him. Just as suddenly as the fog folded in on me, now it began to lift. The sun came through the mist and I could see the far-off tops of trees illuminate, and then the mountains, and once again the birds were singing and the traffic could be heard. God had taken me to a special place that only He and I were. I understood what he was saying, and I agreed with Him.

As the day approached, now Friday, I attempted to reach Cory to see if he had an answer, but there was no response. I tried and still, nothing. I finally accepted that he had turned off his phone to pray, as he had done before.

I readied myself for the time with my friend and the lunch we would share. As I talked with him about the situation, he advised that I say nothing to "rock the boat," but allow Cory to make his own decision without my input. After lunch, we were shopping in an antique mall when finally, the call came.

Cory said, "Well, Meemaw, the decision is made." He related to me the following story. He had called the state university and had asked some outstanding questions. He was very satisfied with their answers and that they were kind and seemed genuinely looking forward to his positive response. He then told me about calling the non-profit ministry and, much to my surprise, he related that the interviewer was accusatory toward him. She stated that she felt he would not be appropriate for the job offered to him. She rescinded the job offer.

She stated she would not hire him at this point. Cory was stunned, shocked, but knew God was in control. We had asked that God make it very clear, and this was done. He attempted to recover the situation, but no explanation was accepted. Cory, though devastated, knew that God had never failed him, and he was at peace with it.

Cory stated, "I am going to stay here, Meemaw, and work downtown." Knowing how long he had dreamed of working for the ministry, I felt a little sick at heart, but he assured me that he was at peace with the decision and praised God for it. He had a chance to make a difference in the secular world.

Who could have ever predicted this outcome? Certainly not me, but God knew all along. God, being who He is, has big plans not just for Cory, but for me, as well. He is the sovereign, omnipotent, omniscient God Almighty. We trust Him and praise Him for an even greater miracle to come.

The Last Whoop

"And God said, Let the earth bring forth the living creature after his kind . . .
and it was so . . . God saw that it was good."
—*Genesis 1:24*

It was the first part of December 2000 when my daughter Kelli and my son-in-law Ben decided to look for just the right dog for my grandson Tad. Ben was a good dad, almost to obsession in those days, and still is to some degree, I guess. Tad, his only child, was Ben's true gift from God. He loves the boy with all his heart, and is thrilled at everything Tad does. He also wanted to give Tad everything within his power to give him.

Tad was one of the cutest kids you could ever imagine. His blonde hair set off his wideset, very large eyes of brown, with eyelashes that would be the envy of any girl around. He was indeed a handsome kid, much in the image of his dad, who had the same attributes. Tad, on the other hand, was in perpetual motion. He was into and out of everything in sight, and just as difficult to handle.

When daycare failed to be tolerable for him and school was coming up, his mom, Kelli, decided rather than to medicate him, he would be homeschooled. Kelli would try diet and natural foods, and instigated everything she could learn to contain his active behavior. Tad had very few friends due to no young children living in his neighborhood. He spent his time in front of the TV, and this was just not acceptable to his parents. They did not want Tad tied down, so perhaps a puppy friend would fill the need. Hopefully, he would run and play with the puppy and would be more fit and healthy because of it. So, the search was on for just the perfect puppy.

Ben asked friends and talked to vets. Both he and Kelli decided the perfect puppy for Tad would be a beagle. These dogs were by breed known to be gentle dogs, and this would be just right for Tad. A calm and gentle dog would balance Tad's very active behavior. Now, to find a breeder who was of high quality and who was known to produce healthy dogs.

It was soon that he discovered a breeder near to home, and visits to the kennel brought a satisfied father and that this was indeed the right decision. Next, Tad was taken to see the puppies and, yes, choose one for his own. The puppies were not old enough to leave the mama, so as Tad picked the one he wanted, he was able to visit the puppy until he could bring it home.

Tad named his puppy Petey, as it was a descendant of the Pistol Pete bloodline. He was a very classic-looking beagle, primarily white with black and saddle-brown puddle-design markings. This puppy could easily be on a postcard or even the cover of a magazine that featured the perfect beagle.

The purchase was made, and now the wait was in order to bring the puppy home. Tad was excited, but Ben was a little concerned that perhaps Tad, being the active, rough little boy he was, might be overwhelming for a puppy. Fortunately, Tad took it all in stride, and he and Petey became constant companions. They watched TV together, and of course Petey shared Tad's food, as well. It was indeed a good match for the boy and the pup.

All was well, until Ben's job moved further north, making it necessary to find a new home. The move was made, but there was no fence for Petey. He had never been kept in the house. Therefore, I, Meemaw, was the only option at the time. You guessed it: Meemaw just inherited a dog.

Petey enjoyed Meemaw's yard and the other dogs: Tippy, a mixed breed, and Furbie, a beautiful buff Pekinese. They ran and played, and whenever Petey chased Furbie, he whooped and whooped as if he was running a rabbit. It was funny to watch, but before long, Petey wanted to go home. He began to run the fence in search of a break so he could get out and go home. It made things worse when Kelli, Tad, and Ben came to visit. He would cry to go with them. Petey was not happy.

His best dog friend, Tippy, knew just what to do. She dug holes under the fence for Petey to escape. Tippy and Furbie never went under the fence, only Petey. He would also climb over the fence if there was anything close enough. His only thought was to get back to where he felt he belonged.

He was well tagged and identified, so he was taken to the veterinary clinic or call there whenever found. It became a real joke, he escaped so often, and then with posters put out and all the search, mysteriously, other beagles appeared in my yard. Every time a beagle was found loose, it was assumed it was Petey, and I would end up with three or more beagles in my yard, none of which were Petey.

Finally, Meemaw decided to build a new home near to where Kelli and Ben lived, and before Petey and the other dogs came to live there, a new fence was installed with sixteen-inch rabbit wire beneath the entire fence to prevent digging out. This worked well, unless someone accidentally left the gate open.

Petey developed an enlarged prostate, which caused him a lot of problems. It was recommended that neutering would sometimes cause the prostate to shrink, and also this would help cure his desire for wandering.

The surgery was carried out without incident, and Petey came home the same day. When I brought him into the house and placed him on the porch for a while, I did not know the builder who was doing work for me had left the gate open. Off went Petey. This was a summer day with temperatures at almost one hundred degrees, and here was the dog just out of surgery running, looking for home.

After much searching by the whole neighborhood, my worker spotted him over a mile away by the power lines near to the highway. He was exhausted and lying down when Bruce picked him up and placed him in the air-conditioned truck. He drank almost a gallon of water, and we put him in an enclosed area and watched him for any signs of problems. He was okay, and within a day or two he was whooping and again searching for a way out.

Approximately eighteen months ago, his weight increased so much, he could hardly walk. He appeared to have developed arthritis, as well, and did not run as much, just whooped and sat around. When brushing him, I noticed a quarter-sized lump in his right belly that was red from him licking it a lot. I put some salve on it and covered it. Not long after that, the lump ruptured, and large clots came out of it with much bleeding. It was diagnosed as a blood tumor, probably malignant from the oversized prostate. He was too weak and old to survive surgery, so possibly he needed to be euthanized. This was not an option to me. I am a pro-life person, and I believe only God has that right, and certainly not me.

It was now winter, and the cold was too much for Petey to be left in the yard, so I brought him in and kept him warm. He liked being inside, and would sit forever if you chose to just stroke his head and tell him he was a good dog. I kept the wound covered with antibiotic ointment and gave him a comfortable bed to sleep on. This posed another problem, because he repeatedly had severe, bloody diarrhea that was terribly smelly and difficult to keep cleaned up. So, with a lot of antiseptic cleansers and smelling, now it was taking a toll on my health, as well. I began to pray for God to either heal him or take his life.

Each morning, I wake at 6:00 a.m. and go to the top level of my yard on a swing, where I have my time with the Lord. Each day, Petey pulled himself up the hill and then would roll down the hill to where the second step was, and then fall down the two bottom steps to the grass and walk back up the ramp to the porch. He was faithful to be there at my feet as I prayed. I reminded the Lord that this dog was faithful and I was being obedient. "Please take him home or heal him."

God reminded me that the dog was being faithful to me, so I should continue to be faithful to care for him. I apologized to God and thanked him for each additional day Petey was able to be there for me. I felt safe in the darkness of the early dawn, because I knew he would bark if there was anything of danger nearby.

Petey began to improve. The tumor diminished and was finally gone. His swelling was gone, and though he looked very bad, he was doing well. He was now running up and down the steps whooping and running "Furbie Rabbit" again, and acted like a teenager. God had healed Petey, I knew it.

As God spoke, "Consider Petey and how much better he is," I testified to my Sunday school class about the healing of Petey. I also complained a little about him waking me at 5:00 a.m. You see, Petey did not know about the time change; he thought he was doing me a favor. That infernal whooping was annoying. But, Petey was back to being Petey. I praised God that he heard the prayers for animals, and that God had shown me a miracle of healing in this faithful dog.

Today, Wednesday, May 5, 2011, 5:00 a.m., Petey whooped. Again, I said, "Oh, Petey, no! It is just five o'clock a.m." Then, Petey whooped four rapid, frantic whoops, and the last whoop as a fading siren winds down. I knew that was not normal for Petey, so I slipped on my robe and got his bone, as I do each day, and made ready for my time with the Lord. I called to him. He did not come. I went to look under the porch and observed something white just at the edge. I quickly ran into the house to get a flashlight as the other dogs stood away observing.

There was Petey. He tried to come to me. He made it far enough to be able to be reached, but he was no longer in that body. Petey had finally made it home.

What a merciful, and mighty, and loving God I serve. He allowed me to see the answer to both of my payers. He gave Petey healing for confirmation to me, and then he answered the desire of Petey's heart: he allowed him to come home. Petey is there with my husband, Richard, stroking his head, I am sure, and Petey, I believe, will be there with the other saints to welcome me when I, too, finally make it home.

Prayer is the answer—the only answer—to all things possible through Christ.

Winter Wonderland

"Thou hast beset me behind and before, and laid thine hand upon me."
—Psalm 139:5

Sometimes the darndest things come into my mind when not really even thinking about a situation. Like yesterday, when my husband and I were riding and looking at all the ice on the trees. What a winter wonderland it represents! Looks like sparkling lights when the sun shines through them. How utterly beautiful God's creation becomes in just of flash of moisture and, of course, the frigid temperature. My mind went into a flurry of remembrance.

Some sixty-seven years ago, I was only eleven years old and we lived in Gainesville, Georgia. We had moved into a garage apartment behind a most beautiful colonial home on Green Street. Mother, my stepdad, my two sisters, and I were cozy and comfortable here. I especially loved living here because the owner was a sweet elderly lady who took a liking to me. I always wanted to play the piano, but never had lessons, so I banged out "Chopsticks" and maybe a few other songs I had learned. The lady always welcomed me into her home and allowed me to play her beautiful grand piano.

The place was not very far from school, so Joyce and I walked to and from school every day. It seemed that somehow the kids knew we were somewhat underprivileged, because they did not readily accept us into their fold, so to speak. Our clothes were not the elite style as some of the others, and I guess we were just not upscale enough to be in a school in this neighborhood. This was not for long, though, because the cold got colder, and then came the storm. Sleet, and snow, and ice everywhere. Hard to walk to school in this, but we did, until that night—that night when the storm came in more ways than one.

My stepdad had been doing well for some time now. He was in partnership with his brother-in-law in a restaurant that was very popular and successful. We were about "to get on our feet" when the storm came. Pops, as we called him, had long been a recovering alcoholic and was very careful to stay away from anything that would set him to fall off the wagon.

This night, he and his partner had a serious falling out, and Pops stopped to get a drink. Knowing full well that he was not able to drink just one, he went down that road again and came in drunk and boisterous. He was slamming things, threatening us kids, and pushing Mother around. Mother knew well that this would lead to someone getting hurt, and that would cause us to be thrown out of the apartment.

Quietly, Mother told us kids to go into the bedroom and put on our clothes, not to say a word, and we would wait until Pops passed out, which he would eventually do. We obeyed, because we knew how violent he could get, and we were scared.

It was at least an hour or so, but seemed like forever, when Mother came into the room and said she would be right back, not to make a sound. Finally, she felt the time was safe and chose to go to the good lady who owned the apartment. Mother told her of our ordeal and asked if she might make a long-distance call on her phone. The good lady said yes and talked to Mother a minute, and the call was made to my uncle to come and get us. Mother felt this was indeed necessary, and so everything was prepared to go. There was ice and snow on the ground, and it was forecast for blizzard conditions.

Understand this was the first storm, but there was a greater one brewing as we readied to leave. My uncle and his girlfriend would leave Marietta and drive to Gainesville to rescue us from a dangerous situation. In those days, there were no highways like we have now, but two-lane roads with no lights or anything to help see how to drive at night. Also, the ice storm was in full bloom now. The trees were covered and beginning to lean over the roadway. I was just thinking, my uncle had to be only twenty-two or twenty-three years old, certainly too young to fear that long, treacherous drive, and with a car with just front and back seats. There were six people in that car and all our belongings.

What a night to travel. I recall we slid all over the road, and at one point a tree limb broke and fell on the road ahead of us. Fortunately, we were unable to travel at the speed limit or faster, or else we would surely have wrecked. There were no other cars on the road, so we were able to pass the brush on the opposite side of the road and continue. The beauty of the ice-coated trees was far exceeded by the danger we were facing. How utterly stupid to get on the roads with this kind of storm, and how strange that anyone would travel that far to get us. I remember well how scared I was. My sisters were asleep in the car seat. Mother and three kids on one small backseat, scrunched together, holding on for dear life.

We made it back to Marietta that night, though I don't remember that part. I don't remember where we went or with whom we stayed. All of that part is a complete blank in this ol' brain. I do indeed remember well that trip and the iced trees, as I saw those similar situations today.

The beauty of a winter wonderland was with me today as the memory became so vivid in my mind. The power is out, but so far the house is still warm, and we look forward to having power again soon. This is one to behold, but truly to take lesson from the past and be ready to survive without power for this time.

I thank my Lord today for the memories that were created that dreadful morning, and know full well that our Lord's hand was upon us as we came through a dangerous time. A miracle to be sure, created and completed by His mighty hand.

$\mathscr{S}$ophisticated Test

"The Lord thy God in the midst of thee is mighty; he will save, he will rejoice over thee with joy; he will rest in his love, he will joy over thee with singing."
—*Zephaniah 3:17*

On or about the first of January 2013, I began a long and difficult time of severe stomach pain, which I felt radiated into the area of my heart. After attempting to resolve the problem with diet and over-the-counter medications, I sought the expertise of my internist. After an extensive history, I was advised that tests needed to be done, first to check out my heart and then my stomach.

I was referred to the hospital to first have an echocardiogram, then complete blood and metabolic screens, both of which were negative for anything except elevated cholesterol and triglycerides, but not exceedingly high. After this, I was referred to a cardiac laboratory for nuclear scan, treadmill, and chemical stress test. These highly sophisticated tests showed only a minor leak in one valve, which was concluded to be within normal limits for someone seventy-six years old and at my activity level. No heart problems were revealed.

I was next scheduled for a barium swallow with MRI contrast included of my abdomen, liver, gall bladder, pancreas, spleen, and lungs. All these tests were reported negative. As the internist shook her head, she suggested that perhaps I needed probiotics to counteract a possible severe acid problem.

This I did immediately. I went to the health-food store and purchased the pure form in capsules, and began a regime of this. My stomach did not improve, nor was it worse by what I ate. I drank milk to attempt to ease the pain with good results sometimes and no results the other. I even purchased an aloe drink, as this was suggested as soothing and healing.

For three days I felt great, and I felt that I had managed to get the right thing to clear my problem. Still occasionally, there was a "pinch" below my left breast that was maybe a two in a one-through-ten ratio of pain. Maybe I was on the mend. At least, that was what I hoped.

On Saturday morning, February 16, 2013, feeling good, my husband and I decided to go to Waffle House for breakfast. I ordered the usual: scrambled eggs with cheese, raisin toast, and a slice of city ham. It tasted really good and I enjoyed the meal very much.

On arriving back home, I took the capsule of acidophilus and then thirty minutes later a couple ounces of aloe drink. Much to my horror, this did not help me, but rather, I began to have severe abdominal pain, almost excruciating. This began to radiate to the sternum and eventually to my left jaw and neck area. It moved on into the left shoulder blade area in the back, and then to the left arm. The area in the left arm felt as though someone had a tourniquet and was trying to squeeze my arm off. The pain was severe.

I called my daughter, who came and took my blood pressure, because my head was ringing and I felt sure the blood pressure was up. It was indeed, probably due to the pain level, I thought. I was urged to go to the ER, but having had all the tests which said my heart was okay, I refused to go. My husband gave me aspirin, and eventually the pain subsided.

I felt sure this was maybe just indigestion and went to bed feeling that I would get up in the a.m. all better. All my pain had subsided. I slept reasonably well, but much to my dismay, I found in the morning I was too weak to get out of the bed. I stayed bedridden for two days with no food, only water, then I gently moved out of bed. Each day I got a little stronger and felt my ordeal was over.

Feeling I was so much better, I chose to go to church on Sunday. I felt too weak to drive myself, so I got my grandson to drive me. While having a conversation with the pastor, once again I developed the drawing in my neck and jaw. This progressed to feeling as though I could not get a breath, and I was frightened. I asked two of our elders to please pray over me, and came home with the understanding that something was surely wrong. I remembered the scripture in James 1 regarding patience and the need for wisdom. I claimed the promise of that scripture and gained wisdom as to having a cardiac catherization. Subsequently, I saw my cardiologist, who stated the likelihood that my heart was not involved, but upon my insistence, scheduled the cath for the following morning.

Much to the shock of my physician, the arteriogram showed one artery, the Dl, was totally blocked, and the LAD was 75 percent blocked. There was also a five-centimeter blood clot at the beginning of this artery branch. I was taken by ambulance to the larger hospital in Atlanta for subsequent repeat cath and repair. Two stents were placed in the blocked arteries, and the thrombosis was successfully removed. After a two-day stay in the hospital, I was returned home with restrictions and medications.

I wanted to write this account, because as a woman, my symptoms were somewhat different and certainly needed to be addressed. We are all so afraid of cancer, and that is a terrible illness; however, more women die of heart attacks every year than any other illness. I hope that this will encourage women to make known these symptoms and to begin to make proper choices regarding food intake and exercise. Also, even if the tests are sophisticated and to the point of less than 1 percent error, you could fit into the less than 1 percent, as did I.

I am thankful to my God for supplying me the wisdom to insist on further testing, which showed my problem. As the operating surgeon said to me, the LAD was close to closing, and that would have been tragic, possibly costing my life. As my original cardiologist said, "She insisted on this test, and because of that, she probably is responsible for saving her own life." No, my God kept me safe and snatched me from the jaws of death. Praise Him in addition to sophisticated tests.

I would be somewhat remiss if I did not also give you the spiritual side of this story. So, here goes. Praise be to God. While I was going through the pain and stomach stress, I was daily praying to the Lord for healing, but quick to let Him know that only if it was within His will. I was willing to suffer the discomfort of the pain and the lousy feeling if it would be of some use to Him. Otherwise, please heal me.

I have been attending a prayer breakfast on Tuesday mornings for some two years now. The study had recently been about the suffering of Jesus and the human suffering we face. I felt that since I had never had to suffer pain, then perhaps this pain would reap a great harvest, both for me and for my God. I was willing to tolerate the pain, but I really wanted to know the source.

I had begun to notice my physical appearance. It seemed that no matter how I tried, I just did not look good. I even went and bought two different foundation makeups, but still could not look better. I felt dragged out and weak, and the least little thing, like putting on eye makeup, caused increased breathing rate. I considered that there could possibly be a crack in my spiritual armor, and that Satan was taking advantage; after all, the tests were all negative. So, something strange certainly could be wrong.

My prayers turned to prayers of praise and thank you's, and I thanked my God for giving me the opportunity to suffer. Upon explaining the fear that I was under a Satanic attack to my pastor on that Sunday morning, he suggested it could be a lesson from God, so not to be too fast to give the credit to Satan. It was then that I felt the smothering that ultimately brought me to the realization that I was not "out of the woods," and asked for prayer. As I talked with two of the church elders, one was the first person I met when I initially came to my church, and the other is a doctor who is a missionary with Doctors Without Borders. Both agreed to come to the altar with me and lay hands on me, and petition God in my behalf. I previously told you about claiming the promise in James chapter 1, and then came the day of the first catherization. I felt I was gradually dying, and as I looked at myself in the mirror, I felt I needed to prepare to meet my maker.

Remembering how Esther prepared for her one night with the king, I, too, wanted to be appropriate to meet my King. I also did not want my family to be embarrassed over my appearance. So, I had my husband drop me at the nail salon to repair my ugly nails and wax my eyebrows. I would be ready for my departure should God choose to take me home.

What a shock it was to me that when the nurse came in to place my IV, I was immediately overcome with fear—so much fear that my teeth were audibly chattering. I was in a nervous jerk.

The young nurse said, "Honey, I am not going to do anything to you except start your IV."

I tried to talk to her, but words could not come. My fear was great. She asked me where I lived, and when I told her, I found that she was my neighbor just a few houses away. What a coincidence! Maybe, but as we talked and shared about our Bible study, and I told the story of when God sat on my swing in the rain to keep my place dry, tears flowed down her face, and mine, and my husband's. With that witness, the fear was cast totally away, and I never felt fear or pain again.

She said, "You were sent here for me today, and I thank you."

I spoke to my Jesus and asked Him to take and hold my hand, and I was sure He was with me all the way. I asked that the problem be found and that it would be fixable. It was indeed found and fixed.

As they initiated the catherization, I kept repeating over and over songs of praise and assurance. I told my God I was in His hands and "thy will be done." God was faithful to me. Even though I felt He was ready to take me home, He chose to grant me mercy. I know He has given me an extension, and I am ready for the task He has for me. I thank Him every moment of every day for His love and support. I asked Him to be my surgeon and to conduct whatever needed to be done. I was and am truly trusting His will in my life. The faulty sophisticated tests were superseded by a merciful and powerful God, and I praise Him for the experience to share with you.

The Motorcycle Crash

"For with thee is the fountain of life: in thy light shall we see light."
—*Psalm 36:9*

I t was a beautiful day. Sun was shining and clear all around. March 21, first day of spring. As I drove, I was thinking about my daughter and the fact that we had not been speaking. After a disagreement with her, I told her, "I am not going to talk to you now, but rather, I am going to give you up for Lent," that way, I would keep my word. I felt that I was always there for her on any occasion, and always put myself on the back burner, regardless of what it was. If I refused to talk to her—not in anger, but for her to have time to feel her loss—then maybe she would be more grateful for all I was doing for her.

Well, I was the one who suffered the loss. I really missed talking to her, whatever the situation was. I thought as I drove, if something were to happen to either of us, how much more traumatic it would be, with us still on the outs. I did not need regrets, nor would she. As I pondered how I could resolve this, I turned onto the "curve road" extension of East Cherokee Drive. The speed limit was twenty-five to forty-five, depending on the severity of the curve. So, I was just cruising along quietly, telling God all about the situation, as if He didn't already know.

I had just crossed over a creek bridge and entered into the curve sections of the road when I saw a motorcycle rounding a big curve approximately two hundred yards ahead. The freshly painted bright-yellow-and-white lines certainly distinguished what was his lane and mine; however, he chose my lane. I slowed down my already slow speed to maybe twenty-five miles per hour, thinking he was just recovering from the curve and would go over into his lane. There were no other vehicles in his lane to prevent him from moving over. For a brief moment, I thought he was moving to his left and my right, but then pulled back into my lane.

At that moment, I knew I had to quickly turn to my left to avoid him. I said, "Oh, God, he's going to hit me," and no sooner than I spoke he crashed into my right front headlight area. I pulled across the oncoming lane—fortunately, no cars were coming—and onto the other side of the road in a flat area near a tree. The cyclist flew off the bike, and bike and rider ended up on the righthand shoulder of the road where there was a cleared area with some gravel.

A car behind me stopped and a lady ran to me to see if I was okay, while two men in a red truck went to check on the cyclist. Feeling that I was okay except terribly stunned, I sat for just a moment thanking God that I was okay. It was at this point I felt God sent me to pray over the man who had hit me, and so I did. As I crossed over the street to get to him, the lady called for police and ambulance.

As I approached the man on the ground, I heard the two men tell him that they were paramedics on their way to work and that he should not try to get up. When I walked over, the two paramedics strangely moved aside, allowing me to lay hands on the young man and pray that God stripes would heal his wounds and comfort his soul. Just as strange, the young man was screaming for me to "Stop, stop!" I knew God was in control, and thanked Him for the opportunity to be a witness to this obviously troubled (besides being injured) young man. I then walked back across the road and sat down by the tree away from the car, lest another car come and hit it. I gave praise to the Lord for His protection.

As I gave my version of the accident, I was given great recall of each second before the crash. Amazingly, I saw my right windshield shatter into what appeared to be a spider-web pattern and a vibrant, electric-white light coming through. The area of the top of my car by the sunroof collapsed into the car. When I looked at my car during the questioning, I was astounded to see no damage of this sort at all. The only damage was the right-front quarter panel and side mirror. My right-front tire was jammed back into the chassis, but that was all. I saw liquid in the middle of the road with the headlight of the bike beside it, and of course the destroyed bike over near where the driver landed.

I was familiar with that "electric-white light." I had seen it once previously, as described in the story regarding our collision with the eighteen-wheelers. I know now, as I did then, this was the Holy Spirit's aura of protection. God was saying to me, "Revonda, this is what would have happened if I had not intervened."

As I am writing this account, it is just as real today, nine months later, as it was that very day. I know God was there, and the young man received the same protection as God was giving to me. I truly believe had he encountered any other car, he would not only have a couple of cuts requiring stitches, but may well have met the Master unprepared. I am certain that had I not turned as quickly as I did, he would have hit me head on, killing us both. However, God gave me the strength and wisdom to do what I did. He saved our lives.

I had a quick examination from the paramedics and refused transportation to the ER. I only had mild pain in my right wrist. Another paramedic showed up on the scene in his personal vehicle and was gracious enough to give me a ride home. It wasn't until about 3:00 a.m. the next morning that I knew I had to see a doctor. My right arm, shoulder, and chest were in considerable pain. I was x-rayed, splinted, and referred to my orthopedist.

Interestingly, my husband wanted to see where the accident happened, and we drove a few days later so I could show him. There are no coordinates at all where I can show him the spot this happened. We have driven up and down the road, looking for the circumstances I described above. No tree, no pull-off area with gravel, nowhere that I can see that far ahead with the bright lines in the road, nothing that is evidence to where this happened. The police report did not describe it correctly either.

So, is it real, or did it really happen? Yes, I know that, because my car was in the shop a good six weeks for repair and I was in a hard cast three months and in soft cast another month. So, where did it happen? Why is it no longer there? I don't know. I only know the story as I have related it to you.

I knew my grandson was anxiously awaiting my arrival to pick him up. I called his cell phone and he, in turn, called his mom, who arranged for someone else to come for him. I then called my husband, but advised for him not to attempt to come to me because I was okay. I also did not want him involved in the traffic mess. I arrived home about thirty minutes later, and related the events to him. I was almost to raving stage at this point, trying to tell everyone who would listen what God had shown me. I am sure those officers thought me somewhat crazy, but I had to tell them of God's mighty power.

I am still today trying to find the place this miracle happened with every time I pass the area. I have even gone when early morning with no traffic and crawled the area, still to no avail. Perhaps it was somewhere offered for God's purpose and not for me to know. I do know, though, that my God is real, and when He says, "I am with you always," I can indeed trust in His Word. He has shown me this, and I will keep it ever close to my heart.

Praise Him always for His faithfulness.

Who Was on the Swing?

"If any man serve me, let him follow me; and where I am, there shall also my servant be: if any man serve me, him will my Father honor."
—John 12:26

Have you ever been in a place where you just didn't feel the presence of God in your life? That place which becomes so lonely that you feel you just can't possibly go through another day? That place where if you can't get a word from Him, you feel absolutely lost? This was where I was at this particular time.

I had always felt that God was with me in all things, because I chose to have Him there. I truly believed that I was walking as close to Him as anyone could, and was indeed in His will. That feeling changed suddenly, without warning, and I felt lost and alone. It happened while studying for our new Bible study life group. As the ten people came to my home to view the new literature, there it was—came out of nowhere: the truth of whether or not I was a follower or just an arduous admirer of Jesus.

We met and had fellowship, going into our prospective week and what we had all been involved in. We ate some good food, laughed, and shared any trials we were facing, as well as many joys. As the conversation began to slow down, our leader, Donald, said, "Let's pray." It was now time for the video we had chosen to study.

Everyone sat quietly. The story was intense and quite moving to all. I could see many tears flow in response to the events that took place, and like so, I, too, was moved. Donald said, "That was very convicting, wasn't it?" All agreed. Then, his wife said she had brought copies of the daily journal for us to consider. Donald asked if there were prayer requests, and when shared, we prayed, and the meeting was closed.

My husband and I cleared the kitchen, placed the chairs back where they belonged, and reflected a bit on what had been shared. We then made ready for bed and a good night's rest. For me, that rest did not come. I could not get the video out of my mind.

I got out of bed and began to read the journal questions and exercises that were suggested for day one. Right away, I knew I was in trouble. When I was asked to close my eyes and picture Jesus in front of me, asking me to follow him, leave everything behind, and take up my cross daily. Suddenly, I felt I was indeed standing in front of Him for real. I could not move, nor could I answer His call. Me, that person who was always talking about Jesus, always sharing scripture, and always ready to pull someone over to His side. Me, of all people, was now hesitating to answer the call. What could possibly be more important than the Lord of my life? Was He indeed the Lord of my life?

As I sat in shock as to seeing the *real* me, I was horrified. I thought to myself that He had just given me the greatest of all gifts in the new, precious husband, whom I adore. Could I give Him my husband? Then, there were my grandchildren and my children, my home, and my friends. Yes, He was indeed number one in my life, but I wanted numbers two, three, and four also.

About that time, my husband realized I was not in the bed and got up to check on me. He asked, "Are you okay?"

I answered that I couldn't sleep and I would be back to bed shortly. I knew Jesus had to be disappointed in me, but I also knew He was aware of my condition. This came as no surprise to Him at all. I felt terrible. *Who am I, anyhow?* I thought. The Master of the Universe, King of Kings, and Lord of Lords invited me to follow Him, and I was hesitant to give Him an answer. I felt defeated and slowly moved back to bed for a continued sleepless night.

Wednesday was a full day. I did not even go to meet Him on my swing, as I did every morning. Instead, I attempted to do everything myself. Well, you know what happened then. Certainly, nothing went right at all.

My daughter had to get the emission test on her car, which had just been repaired. It did not pass the emission test. The long drive to and from her house was for nothing. With gas prices as they were, that was such a waste. She would have to make the trip again.

I was out of sorts, and it seemed that my husband and I could not agree even on what or if we wanted to eat. Everything was a mess. I tried to pray, but words did not come. I attempted to read my devotional, but my mind was so scattered that I could not remember what I had read. This thing had to be settled.

I continued on to the next part of the exercise that had set me in such a whirlwind. This time I had to list what I might withhold from Jesus. Then, I had to compare those things or that person to Jesus. What did He bring to me, and what did the others bring to me? Needless to say, there was no comparison. But, I was still in limbo.

At this point, I decided to read chapter two and see if it would give me any insights. It did indeed. It seemed that the writer had anticipated exactly what I was feeling. Truly, this was written just for me. I was not the only one who had this reaction; I was one of many. Mostly, all felt the same. The true were few and far between. That gave me some peace about my feelings, but I still felt conviction. I continued with the questions and answered them as I could. I was beginning to understand why I had been put in this situation. I had to know what I would do.

Finally, at the close of the day, I knew beyond a shadow of a doubt that there was no one who could compare to Him. He was worth everything and everyone in my life. I would indeed be willing to give it all to Him. I had finally been able to define the relationship I had with my Lord.

Now, I had to repair that relationship. I knew Jesus was always there, but for some reason my guilt in all of this had separated me from Him. I was not able to feel His presence, smell His essence, nor hear His voice. I had really messed up.

I returned to my swing the next day and spent time praising Him and talking out the situation I had put myself into. I told Him I felt separated. I needed assurance. I needed confirmation that I had not so damaged our relationship that He had fled from me. The scripture "I will never leave you nor forsake you" kept playing over and over in my mind.

It was now Friday morning, a rainy day, and many clouds rolled over. It was about 6:30 a.m., and I climbed out of my bed and put on my robe and boots to go out on the swing to be with Him. Strangely enough, it seemed that always, even though it was raining, it would miraculously cease just long enough for me to meet with Him.

Today, as I walked out and covered my head with the blanket I always used, the drops of rain were just to the point of a drizzle. I felt I wanted to go anyway, regardless of the rain. As I walked across the deck, I looked up to the swing on the hill. I noticed my little dog was sitting in front of the swing just to the side, intently looking at the swing. I chuckled inside and said to myself, "She is wondering where I am. She is expecting me to be there."

As I came closer, she questioningly looked first at me, then at the swing, almost puzzled-looking. I walked to the swing, arranging the blanket so that I would not sit on the wet, when I noticed a very strange thing. The whole swing was wet with the droplets of rain, except for the center of the swing, where I would always sit. That portion of the swing was completely dry, as if someone had been sitting there keeping that spot dry. I said, "Thank you, Lord, for keeping the swing dry for me."

I sat down, and my eye was immediately drawn to my Japanese pink magnolia. This had bloomed just before Easter, and now I was greatly surprised to see that it was again full of beautiful pink blooms.

I had my prayer time and praise time. My husband came onto the deck. He was never up this early, but he spoke and said, "Hello," and quickly went in out of the rain. I was not being rained on at all. I finished my time with the Lord that day and was relieved to know He was not mad at me. Rather, I had received a great lesson in faith.

I have had much time to think about what happened and why, but mainly, I really need to put this into proper prospective. When it happened, I just took it so very matter of fact, almost as if I expected it, but that certainly was not the case. Perhaps I was in a sort of shock or whatever, but what an amazing, wonderful thing had occurred. Someone had to have been sitting on that swing; that is the only explanation. No one was there that my eyes could see. However, my little dog, Furbie, certainly was looking at someone or something. When I took my place on the swing, she continued to go across the yard, as if to follow someone. At one point, she stopped, looked up, and whimpered a bit, as though she saw something or someone move upward.

Now I ask, "Who was on the swing?" I choose to believe that my Lord sat there and waited for me, keeping my place dry, for no other reason than to give me assurance that He loves me and will never leave me.

Again, who was on the swing? Would the Master of the Universe, King of Kings, Lord of Lords, my Savior and friend take time out of His busy day to show me such favor? I believe He did indeed, and I will treasure that moment for the rest of my days.

He is the beginning and the end, the first and the last, the Olef and Tav. My one and only God, forever.

${\mathscr{A}}$ngel Unaware

"Be not forgetful to entertain strangers: for thereby some
have entertained angels unawares."
—*Hebrews 13:2*

I had read the scripture that you should be careful, because you may be entertaining angels unaware, but never did I think that would be true for me. I witnessed what I believe to be just that during a real crisis with my husband in 1997.

Richard had developed a fever that kept going higher and higher. In this condition, I found that I was unable to get medication down him by mouth. I knew that when the fever got too high, he automatically began to have an apnea attack, which would stop his breathing for nearly a minute to a minute and a half at a time. So, when after much effort in attempting to lower his temperature failed, I felt he had to be taken to the emergency room quickly. I knew, of course, this can stress the heart, and could also cause another respiratory and cardiac arrest.

After bathing him to attempt to cool him, I awaited the ambulance and paramedics. I gave them very strong and specific instructions as to what had to be done, relaying the previous year when he had suffered the arrest and was pronounced dead for thirteen minutes. So, this was not something to be taken lightly; it was indeed a life-and-death emergency. They assured me that they understood completely. I gave them the information for them to have his previous admission pulled and ready.

I put together some of his medications and set forth to follow the ambulance there. Upon arrival in the emergency room, I was taken to the admissions office to sign papers. Richard was taken on to the back and into a room. I protested that I needed to be with him, but they insisted that I complete the registration papers.

Although he had been in the hospital recently, all the information had to be reset, just in case there had been a change in anything. I insisted that there were no changes, but again, it had to be done all over, as if it had never been done before. At least twenty minutes had passed, and now I could be taken back to where he was.

Much to my surprise, there he was, oxygen in his nose, totally unconscious. There was no one with him and nothing was being done for him. I went immediately to the nurses' station to complain, and was told they had a lot of patients, and they would be there as soon as they could. I protested and insisted they get a doctor there right now. I relayed that he had had a respiratory and cardiac arrest only a year previous under similar circumstances and was pronounced dead for more than thirteen minutes. I insisted that he would again go into respiratory arrest if this temperature was not alleviated quickly.

I received no concern for my effort and was told, "As soon as we can, we will be there." I was very fearful as to the outcome, and knew God had to be called. As I proceeded to return to the room where he was still comatose, I pulled up a chair, put my head on him, and began to pray. Then, I reached into my purse and found a David Wilkerson *Promise Book*, and started to read out loud. One by one, I read the promises of God, which covers all emergencies, and calling upon the angels for assistance.

I had not previously noticed that there was another person in this room. The room was divided with a chrome rail next to the ceiling, which supported a cream-colored curtain to give privacy. This was pulled, and I was unaware of anyone else in the room until now.

Out of the quiet, a very deep, masculine voice spoke to me and asked, "Ma'am, what is that you are reading from?"

I answered, "David Wilkerson's *Promise Book*."

Then the voice replied, "Well, I believe the Word says that when two or more are in same accord that God himself is right there with them, and I am agreeing with you in this."

I continued to read: John 3:16 "For God so loved the world, that he gave his only begotten Son, that whosoever believeth in him shall not perish, but have everlasting life," Psalm 23 "Though I walk through the valley of the shadow of death, I will fear no evil: for thou art with me," Mark 9:23 "Jesus said unto him, If thou canst believe, all things are possible to him that believeth." On and on, one after the other, speaking God's promises, believing that this was the only thing I could do. No one was coming to help; only the Lord could do anything about it.

Eventually, a nurse walked into the area where the other voice had come from and asked if he needed anything, and he replied, "No." Just then, there was a lot of hustling around the halls. It seems that there had been an accident out on the highway and a tomato truck had overturned. Several cars had wrecked, and they were bringing in the wounded. Mostly cuts and bruises, but blood is taken care of first, it seems.

By this time, Richard's breathing had become more and more shallow, and his temperature was now registering 106 degrees. I was in tears. No one was listening to my cry for help. Then, the voice said to the nurses, "I am just waiting for a prescription, so if you need this room, I can wait outside in the hall."

The nurse thanked him. I put my head back down on Richard and began to cry out to the Lord, "Please help us, Lord!"

I felt a hand on my shoulder, and the voice said, "Ma'am, I would like to pray for you and your husband, if I may."

I said, "Please do, sir."

The man began to pray, and I was totally covered with chills as he spoke peace, and joy, and healing over us both. When he said, "Amen," he said, "Ma'am, I will continue to pray for you and your husband until I am told everything is all right."

Just then, I lifted my head to say thank you, and much to my surprise, I saw an amazing thing. This was the dirtiest, smelliest, most frightful-looking man I had ever seen. He was covered with tattoos, had stringy, dark hair that somehow stuck together, rings in his nose and ears, and snaggle-toothed. He was wearing a captain's cap, which was really dirty, and a leather vest that showed his hairy chest, which was quite visible and smelly. Once again, I thanked him, but did not, under any circumstances, want to hug this guy. I thought to myself if I had seen this man at night on the street, I would certainly have run the other direction.

While I was demeaning this very nice and spirit-filled man under my breath, I heard the Lord say, "Careful, you may be entertaining an angel unaware." With that, I ran to the door of the room and looked down the hall. He was nowhere in sight. I asked the people in the hall which way he may had gone. No one saw him. Then, I asked the nurse who had come to get his prescription. She didn't know where he went.

Suddenly, a flurry of action began. Two doctors and three nurses were all there and began to work on Richard, bathing him, giving him IV fluids and medication, and within just a few minutes, Richard opened his eyes. Not today did he die again. Not today did we have to admit him to the hospital. He was suddenly okay, and was shortly dismissed to be taken home.

Was this indeed an angel in disguise? I do not truly know. I only know the Lord told me he could well have been. I believe he indeed was an angel.

Careful, you may be entertaining an angel yourself and never be the wiser. Once again, God came through for us, and we again today praise Him for His omnipotence, His sovereignty, and for just being who He is: a mighty God, who is ever present and all knowing.

God's Minute Helicopter

"All things were made by him; and without him was not any thing made that was made."
—John 1:3

Recently, during one of our Bible-study meetings at our home, one of our participants asked for prayer for her son. As with most mothers, she had genuine concern for his safety. He had recently completed officers' candidate school and was shortly to be deployed to Afghanistan. This was a time when there was especially hot unrest there, and many young American soldiers had lost their lives. She, being a committed Christian, had always put her children into God's protective care. She trusted the Lord with all her heart and mind, and now she wanted the assurance that he was adequately covered.

Her prayer request was taken by the group and noted, so that we would remember to honor these requests. As our group prayer ended and we made departure to our homes, all hugged one another and assured that their requests would be seriously remembered to continually be lifted to the Lord.

The following week, we all returned to finish the last chapter of Galatians and to discuss what the apostle Paul was trying to teach us, this being that we must not be pulled by world requirements, but to trust completely in the finished work of the cross. As we commented on how this amazing book had impacted our individual lives, the mother once again spoke regarding her son. With holy praise, she related that her prayer had indeed been answered. Her son not only had not been deployed, but had received a commission to be trained to be a helicopter pilot. This had been his heart's desire for a long time.

She gave thanks to God for answering her prayers and thanked us for being participants with her in these prayers. We all rejoiced with her and praised God for His mighty response, remembering His promise that where two or more are gathered in same accord, that He would be present with us. We believed this promise and joined together with that assurance.

Today, this story became vivid to me as I sat giving praise to my God for all His wonderful blessings and creations. As I sat on my swing, I observed a beautiful hummingbird just ahead of me sipping nectar from the blossoms of my mimosa tree. It was so tiny and so colorful, yet so amazing in its ability to maneuver from side to side and up and down, but mostly, how it could stand still in the air. My mind traveled back to what it must have been like in the beginning, and how our Lord had created this small bird, how the very concept of air travel must have been impacted by this small wonder. God gave His most miraculous creation, man, a vision of how this could be put into a highly technological feat for use in air travel.

Scientists and technologists boast of their inventions and their technological accomplishments, and yet the Word assures us that there is nothing new under the sun. It is well known that the Black Hawk helicopter is considered one of this nation's finest defense weapons. It is also known that the people who take great pride in their design of this helicopter probably rarely consider that the design was created at the foundation of the world by the chief of all inventors, our Lord. In John 1:3, we are told that "All things were made by him: and without him was not any thing made that was made."

Behold the hummingbird, how it is able to whisk across the sky and suddenly stop in midair to plot its course and then forge forward again. So amazingly unique that it escapes all possibility of being recreated as such. What a mighty and wonderful God our creator is in all things, big and small. The intricate wonder of tiny wings and feet, and the long, pointed beak, its rudder, to balance the complete work of a thoroughly marvelous engineering feat. Tiny bones, and tiny feathers and muscles and nerves, with the blood vessels so tiny, and such tiny organs as heart, lungs, brain, and all. What an unbelievable creation, so beyond our ability to comprehend this wondrous hummingbird.

Yes, the helicopter is indeed an amazing machine full of all sorts of technological parts, wires, fuses, etc. However, none are so miraculous and so amazing as God's minute helicopter. More and more, nature speaks of His sovereignty and power. We need only to open that eye that He gives us to see His miraculous creations.

I urge you to take the time to allow Him to show you His wondrous works, and be blessed to acknowledge His uniqueness as the one and only God of the Universe, the God who can take a most sincere prayer from a mother and bring forth a miracle result, create a living being with all the proprieties of a tiny bird, and still be with us at all times.

How great is our God, our Father, the Master of the Universe? He is worthy to be praised.

Gift of God's Love

"The heavens declare his righteousness, and all the people see his glory."
—*Psalm 97:6*

Today is March 29, 2010. Today I received a wonderful gift from my Father. This really goes back to approximately two years ago, when I visited a local nursery to purchase additional shrubbery. I had cleared an area in my front yard and planted tulips, daffodils, pansies, and other annuals, but I really wanted a redbud tree to put at the top area. After shopping for the aforementioned plants, I went to the area of trees and bushes, only to find that a redbud tree was too expensive for me to buy.

I went home and planted the other plants, but I truly wanted to put a redbud at the top. I was disappointed that they were so expensive, and began to think of something else that would do just as well, but not be as expensive. I first tried a flowering cherry. It died. I then bought a dogwood, and it did not make it, either. I was beginning to think that the area must not be good for planting a bush or a tree, and left it clear.

I went through that summer and thought no more about the redbud or any other tree, and then, near the fall, when things were beginning to go away, much to my surprise, a small upshoot appeared with heart-shaped leaves. I was really surprised about this, which I should not have been, because my Father has often given me little gifts before. I remembered that at the time I saw the expensive one in the previous year that I had said to my God, "Lord, that is too expensive, so I will choose something else." Well, just as I have heard this kind of "un-request" from my children and given to them the desire of their heart, like so, my Father had given me the tree, which grew like a weed, but never did it produce any blooms. I was beginning to believe that perhaps I was mistaken and that this was not a redbud from God, but just a wild tree.

Today, as I completed my time with the Lord, I decided to go out and prune back some of the long shoots from my bushes, and ultimately went to do the same to the tree. I had really thought it was growing too big, and not having any flowers, I might just choose to cut it down. Much to my joy, as I approached the tree, there on the branches were numerous small buds ready to break forth. I was so excited that I began to cry and lift my hands to Heaven in thanks to my Father for this wonderful gift.

I know that this may seem trivial to some of you, but every gift He has afforded me has come after a period of obedience, almost as if He is rewarding me. I have such joy in my heart today. I could not wait to share this miracle with my friends and certainly with the group at my prayer breakfast.

I believe that God, as our Heavenly Father, often gives us miraculous gifts, if only we look for them. He is so good and wants to please us, and how we should want to please Him. He is so wonderful and so loving, and I praise Him for who I know Him to be, especially my Daddy, my friend, and most of all, my God.

$\mathscr{A}$ Very Definite Healing Miracle

"In my distress I called upon the Lord . . . He heard my voice out of his temple, and my cry came before him, even into his ears."
—Psalm 18:6

T hings around our house had been somewhat peaceful for a while. We had been through a bit of a hassle when my daughter found she was pregnant with her fourth child. Having three children and feeling that that was enough, this pregnancy was rejected by her husband. He felt somewhat overwhelmed with such a big family and all so quickly, even though he was as much responsible as my daughter.

It seemed that this pregnancy came right about the same time as "the right to choose" became a big campaign issue. My son-in-law and his parents were great supporters of this issue, and I was faced with the possibility that this baby may well be denied his right to life. Prayer was indeed the answer, and I began a constant attitude of prayer on behalf of my unborn grandchild.

The issue was soon resolved when my daughter had her doctor's appointment and found that she was further along in her pregnancy, making termination a moot option. I praised God for this report and awaited the birth of my grandson. Though things became difficult for my daughter, in that her husband totally rejected this baby, a planned dedication of the child was scheduled.

Several weeks prior to this event, my son was driving home when he was rear-ended and sustained a pretty severe whiplash injury. This injury resulted in a complete loss of his voice. Thinking this would resolve itself, he delayed any further consultation. After many doctor visits, it was determined that his loss of voice could only be corrected surgically. This was subsequently scheduled, and my son awaited the time when he could be off from work to have this surgical procedure. Since the insurance companies were fighting over the accident, an attorney had to be sought to support my son's interests. Well, a goodly settlement was scheduled to be recommended, and my son prepared for the surgical procedure.

It was the Sunday when my grandson was to be dedicated. Since he was named after my son, it was certainly appropriate for my son to be there to support his sister and namesake. I had spoken to the minister prior to the service, and asked him to pray for my son's healing, that the Lord would do a miracle and the dangerous surgery would not be necessary. As the service proceeded, we were all asked to come to the altar for the presentation of the child to be dedicated. We, as a family, stood before the altar. The anointing of the child was done, after which the minister went to each family member present and laid hands on each. When he reached my son, knowing that he had an issue of health, the minister anointed his head and prayed over him.

The service ended with everyone going to celebrate the dedication and then to individual homes. At this point, my son still had no voice and was still scheduled to see his attorney and, subsequently, his doctor.

My son awakened the following morning with his voice totally restored.

My son was healed that day, and hasn't stopped talking since. The rather large settlement went down the drain, but no surgery was required. He came to the church to support his sister and namesake, and God rewarded him with total healing.

We rejoice in hearing my son's very electric laughter and joyful voice. We praise God for such a blessing and give Him all the glory. Let me also state here and now that this child was anointed that day, too. He has knowledge that is far beyond his years and a trust in God that shows through to others who meet him.

Return to Grace

"Restore unto me the joy of thy salvation; and uphold me with thy free spirit."
—Psalm 51:12

ometimes it seems we, as Christians, become so wrapped up in the everyday life that we lose our way. God has made it very clear in all things and all circumstances that He will never leave us nor forsake us, but we may very well leave and forsake Him. Certainly not intentionally, nor with forethought, but just caught up in the world and busy lives. This had been the case for me, and I was walking on my own and not necessarily where God would have me to walk. In the midst of this carnal condition, a miracle unfolded that involved several lives in a most profound way.

My daughter Jenna had become engaged, and stated her desire to be married in the church in which her dad and I had served the Lord. I inquired of the church hostess as to procedure, and reserved the sanctuary, the organist, and put into motion the plans for the wedding. We had a wonderful minister at that time, but not one I knew well at all. I requested that my nephew be allowed to conduct the ceremony. I was told that it was tradition and within the church rules that the presiding minister be the one who conducted marriages. I asked if my nephew could be a part of the service and was told that he was welcome to do so.

We had the rehearsal, and everything was set for the next day and the wedding. Allow me to insert here that until this time I had not been attending any church, and certainly not this, my home church, reason being my lifestyle was not acceptable to my church "friends" and family. So, I decided that if I was going to use the church for my daughter's wedding, that surely I was expected to attend church. This I did, though reluctantly.

I had contacted my nephew and told him of the church's tradition, but asked him to be a part of the service by presenting the love chapter. As I mentioned the name of the minister, I was greatly surprised to learn that my nephew not only knew of this minister, but this minister was the first to allow my nephew to preach as a very young man. What a strange coincidence? Not exactly: all by plan, of course.

As the wedding party arrived, so did my nephew. When he went behind the choir loft to change into his robe, he suddenly came face to face and recognized the senior pastor and his old friend. The two men embraced and both sobbed with joyful excitement. What a wonderful reunion this was for the two men of God. Until that moment, neither knew who the other pastor would be. What a wonderful story would unfold!

It seems that the senior pastor was praying for God to bring him the right place to serve. When he was told to go to a little church in a very small town, this was just not what he had hoped for, and continued to deny the calling. He really wanted to serve as a minister missionary in another country. As he continued to pray and trust God for an appointment, the small church and town kept being offered. After much prayer and asking for understanding, his then-young wife said, "There is always the little church."

Finally, he accepted to go serve in the little church of no more than a dozen members, but one of those members was a young twelve-year-old boy who had been called to preach. The pastor talked to him, and after much prayer and counseling, the young boy was given the pulpit to preach. This opportunity set forth a flurry of speaking times for the young minister. As time passed, the senior pastor was given a new appointment and the young minister lost track of him. Not until this wedding had the two been in contact.

The wedding service went beautifully well and was a blessing to all who attended. It also set up a time for the senior pastor to be asked to come and deliver a message in the young minister's (now bishop's) church. By this time, I had become active in my church again, and went to be present for that blessed occasion. You see, the senior pastor never was appointed to go abroad, but rather pastored several large churches. The young minister-bishop became a world evangelist and carried God's Word to many nations, published several books, and was responsible for many souls throughout the world. I, too, received a calling and was anointed to teach, and am still fulfilling that anointment today.

God has such miracles just behind the scenes, even when we don't know what is going on. He has a plan that is carried out in wonderful ways. I hope that this will encourage you to trust Him, because our greatest dreams may be fulfilled through someone to whom we have been an influence. God is omniscient, and I am thankful that He is in charge, thankful that He has returned me to His grace.

$\mathcal{A}$ Very Unprecedented Pie

"O, taste and see that the Lord is good: blessed is the man that trusteth in him".
—*Psalm 34:8*

It was the last day before school was to begin again for my four grandchildren. I was staying with them while their mom was in her final two weeks of college courses and would not be home before lunch was over. I questioned the kids as to what they wanted Meemaw to prepare for them to eat. After much difference of opinion, I opted to make chicken salad and a pot of chicken and dumplings. They could eat the chicken salad in sandwiches for their lunch, and the dumplings would be for their dinner. Mom would not have the chore of preparing anything and get them ready for school the next morning.

As the food was completed, the kids started searching the cabinets to find a suitable dessert. When they found nothing they particularly wanted, I offered to make my mother's recipe for chocolate pie. This had always been a favorite for the whole family, and I had all the ingredients, so that was my decision.

My granddaughter was quite interested to learn to cook and wanted to help with the pie, so I began instructing her on each step as we continued. First, I explained the ingredients, then one-step process at a time. We placed the milk in the saucepan with the cocoa and salt, and brought it to a low boil. I instructed her on how to separate the yellow of the eggs from the white and set aside for meringue. We then beat the yellow with milk added and a tablespoon of cornstarch to thicken to pudding consistency. All looked really good.

We turned the pudding off and continued to make the pie crust. At this point, she had become a little bored and walked into the next room. I completed the crust mixture and rolled it out appropriately and placed into the pie pan. In the confusion, I quickly got the saucepan of pudding and poured into the crust to be cooked. Just as I poured into the crust, I shockingly remembered the crust had to be baked first before pouring the pudding mixture into it. I was horrified that I had done such a silly thing.

About that time, my granddaughter returned to the kitchen, at which point I had to admit to her of my mistake. The pie crust was ruined, of course, and another would have to be made. I quickly poured the pudding mixture back into the saucepan to wait for the crust. As I poured the spoiled crust out of the pan, chocolate got on my fingers and of course, as all cooks do, the fingers immediately went to my mouth to get just a taste of the beautiful chocolate mixture. No sooner than my finger touched my tongue, an unexpected, terrible truth was evident: I had not only failed to cook the crust first, but I had failed to combine the cup of sugar that was required to make the pudding mixture eatable.

The taste was awful, bitter, and almost to gag point. How could this be, after all the years of making this recipe, and after having made two just the day before? I somehow failed to include the sweet sugar flavor to my pie. I was devastated, to say the least, and I began to cry.

My youngest grandson began to console me, saying, "It's all right, Meemaw. We don't need pie, anyway. Please don't cry. It's okay, really. Isn't it, guys?"

Well, the others showed disappointment, and my granddaughter made it worse by laughing at my mess. After all was said and done, the pie was fixed with a new crust. I did indeed add the sugar to the pot of chocolate mixture and placed it into the baked shell.

Now, another problem: I had beat the egg whites until stiff peaks when I realized I had used every grain of sugar in the pudding, and there was none to sweeten the meringue. So, being the resourceful person I am, I added some sugar substitute. This made the meringue a bit flat and really didn't do well. The pie tasted really good, I am told, and all was eaten, but the damage to my ego was severe. I was totally down, to the point that I left for home immediately when my daughter came in without even cleaning up my mess.

As I drove home, I was feeling old and confused. Was I just a victim of old age, and was I going to start not being able to do things I had always done before? I was really "whipped," and the ol' devil was having a good laugh.

Finally, I began to laugh at myself and deny the old spoiler victory over me. I turned my eyes to Jesus and told Him that this type of thing didn't happen just for no reason, but that I was sure there was a very good lesson I needed to learn here. As I searched my spirit for an explanation, I felt the following truth come to the surface: "the best of things are never complete without Him to sweeten it."

Although the pudding looked perfectly right, to taste, it was all wrong. The sweet ingredient was necessary to make it really true pie. Like so, all the events of our life can feel and look like good, but without Him to sweeten the pot, those events are useless for our lives. Also, there is a definite order that God has set into place. When we defer from that order, like the pie crust, we become useless. We must heed the directions He gives to us in His Word and allow Him to fulfill the plan. In His own time and His own way, He directs us to perfection that can be enjoyed by all who observe our actions and care about us.

Yes, it was a good thing I wanted to do for my grandchildren, but a better thing to receive a lesson at my old age that can be shared with them. Life is fragile. We must handle it with prayer, trust, and in all ways, obedience. Jesus is the sweet nectar that makes our life something to consume with pleasure. Had I followed the directions instead of my memory, I could have avoided defeat. If I follow His directions for my life, I will find that Jesus is joy and a way-maker in all things.

A very unprecedented pie indeed, but a very true lesson in life.

God at Work

"Surely goodness and mercy shall follow me all the days of my life:
and I will dwell in the house of the Lord for ever."
—Psalm 23:6

As I sit in my swing, I notice so very much of the completed work of my God: the beautiful roses in my garden, with their sweet perfume that drizzles through the morning air; the intricate workmanship of the blossom of the mimosa tree, with its essence of sweet, peach-like aroma; and then the amazing formation of the clouds in the perfect shade of blue sky, all put into place with one mighty stroke. I am thoroughly in awe when I observe the tiny feet of a wren as it grasps a small branch upon which to stand, and then the ability to fly no more than six inches off the ground with jet-propelled speed. How great is my God? How mighty is He? His work and creativity are so far beyond my ability to understand, but yet given for me to behold. How special are these gifts for such an unworthy world of people?

He has told me that I am "beautifully and wonderfully made," that He "knows the number of hairs on my head," and that He "feeds and clothes the birds of the air, and so how much more will He take care of me," and most of all, that He "will never leave me nor forsake me." He has given me a love letter to know who He is and what He has done, and given me a design to follow. His work has spanned over centuries of wars and rumors of wars, and still exists for us all to see. Today, He allowed me to see Him physically at work through the nature He has created.

I had come to the swing at about 7:00 a.m. I placed the Mexican-made blanket over my head, walked up the steps to my swing, and sat down. I reached into my pocket for a treat to give to my two dogs as they faithfully sat at my feet, and sang the little chorus, "Lord, I thank you for the morning." Once again, today I observed the robins as they alternately sat upon a nest in the thick of my jasmine bush that drapes poetically over the cast-iron arbor. I had watched these birds as they meticulously built the nest. They brought one straw at a time over many days, and then after the rain, picked up pieces of mud and glued the straw together. They got into the nest and wriggled to put just the right shape to place eggs there, and then to sit patiently on those eggs until they were hatched. Today, the hatched offspring were ready to be fed.

As I sat and praised my God for all the wonderful things He had created and allowed me to witness, then He began His work for me to see. I watched the daddy bird scout the ground and then peck it to call up a worm. He grasped it in his beak and started toward the nest. He flew like a rocket over the ground to a nearby crepe myrtle bush, stopped for a moment on a top branch, and cautiously looked from side to side, making sure there was no predator in the area. He then flew to the top of a rose bush on the other side of the arbor, then back onto the ground, pecking at the ground again, as though he was just getting himself some breakfast. He sleuthed out a safe path, and finally moved to the top of the arbor, and carefully moved through the thick branches.

As he came near the nest, the mother bird moved off the nest and flew out the other side, as if to be a decoy for daddy bird's effort. Then, he jumped to the side of the nest, and I observed two wide-open beaks pulsating up and down as the daddy robin placed food into each mouth. You did not see heads; it appeared these were just all beaks opened wide to be fed.

As he completed his task, he waited, and the mama bird followed the carefully laid path to return to the nest, their safe haven. How strange yet wonderfully set forth by my God! What an amazing picture of a marriage! One male bird and one female bird joined together as life partners, each performing their very purpose and design, as He had made them to be: different, yet joined together to fulfill the plan God had set for their lives.

It was at this precise moment that I saw God at work—at work through His physical creation to demonstrate to me His workmanship in the path He has forged for my life. He has cautiously set forth a path for me to follow that is free of snares and stumbling blocks. My only input is to follow His lead. I must trust that He, like the daddy robin, is keeping a protective eye out for any evil that could befall me. As long as I walk on the path He has set forth for me, in the words of the psalmist, I can "fear no evil, for thou art with me." He "leads me beside the still waters" should I thirst. He "leadeth me on the path of righteousness." He "restoreth my soul." He is my shepherd, and I have everything I need.

Now that He has shown through His physical work using His creation, the robin, to reveal to me Him in action, I understand the spiritual work He is doing in my life. What I could not see, He has chosen to demonstrate to me that I may know Him, trust Him, and feel free to follow Him without fear of what lies ahead. The plan was put into place at the foundation of the world. He knew me then as He knows me now. There is nothing He does not know about me.

I call on Holy Spirit to be with me and guide my steps on the path that has been set forth for me. If my Lord chose to show me this miracle, then "surely goodness and mercy shall follow me all the days of my life: and I will dwell in the house of the Lord for ever."

$\mathscr{A}$ Rough Cut

"I can do all things through Christ who strengthens me."
—Philippians 4:13

S pring had sprung, and all was beginning to bloom, and I was antsy to get going, too. I, just three years into my seventies, was healthy, feisty, and capable. I had been doing my own fixer-uppers for years, and the ladder, skill saw, and drill were my friends. I loved to make things over and enhance the beauty of it all—that is, for my personal taste—and many thought I was amazing. I thought so, too. Yard work was fun, and I made my yard the talk of the neighborhood. It was indeed pretty. So, another season of getting it ready was here.

As I contemplated what was next on the outside, I saw that the grass in the backyard was getting to the level that cutting was needed. I, in turn, pulled out the ol' mower to make ready to cut. I checked the spark plug, cleaned it a bit, emptied the gas, and checked the oil. All was well, and I was ready to begin. I put on some old shoes, sun bonnet, gloves, and old clothes for yard work, and now to begin.

Reaching over, I pulled the start cord and pulled it again—no start. I stood there a moment, pumped the little rubber ball to get the gas into the carburetor, and I pulled again. *Putt putt*, but no start. I stood back and, being the believer that I am, I spoke to my Lord, "Now, Lord, if you want me to get this grass cut, you are going to have to help me start this mower." Believing, once again I pulled the cord, and right away we were putting along. So far, so good.

The lower part of the yard was pretty level and would usually pose no problem cutting, but I found after only about twenty minutes, I was breathing fast, and decided to take a rest. I went into the house to get a glass of cool water and a cloth to wipe my forehead, and returned to mow some more. Twenty minutes more and I stopped again. I told the Lord, "I guess I am getting to be an ol' lady. You will probably have to help me finish."

Finally, the lower part of the yard was complete, and I was ready to go to the upper half, which was not so level and more difficult terrain. I pushed the mower up the hill and went across one and then two rows, and wow, I was exhausted. I sat down upon the swing that I chose to be my meeting place with the Lord daily. I rested and talked to the Lord for a few minutes, and then got up to go again.

As I walked over to the mower, my dogs came to beg for some attention. I stopped and talked to them for a moment, and then went on to the mower to once again pull that cord and get going. I looked around at the yard ahead and the higher grass than below. I said, "Lord, this is not going to be so easy, so may I please have some of your strength to do this?"

I pulled the cord and the mower started right away, and then the Lord spoke to me, saying, "Don't forget to push the red lever." Suddenly, shocked, I remembered I have a self-propelled mower. Needless to say, I had quite a laugh on myself. What a difference, and how easy the mowing was now. I whizzed through that part of the yard with such efficiency and grace, you would not believe. I had forgotten the mower was self-propelled and mowed all that lower section of grass without the self-propel on.

As I look back on that day, it brings a chuckle to me and a deep joy to know that my Lord can and will answer my plea for assistance with such a gentle spirit so as not to embarrass or belittle me. I continued to mow my lawn the rest of that summer, and always remembering how my Lord had reminded me of the most simple things. To get it done, I know that "I can do all things through Christ who strengthens me." A rough cut became the smoothest of cuts with His direction.

Praise be to my Lord for all that He does for me.

He Is at Peace . . . Wrong!

"Help me, O Lord."
—Psalm 70:1

Over the years, I have often heard people state that someone just went to sleep and is at peace. Is this always the case when this is said? Well, that is exactly what would have been said had I not been right there at the time. This miracle happened somewhere around 2000, I would say. It is kind of hard to remember all the dates, but very vividly the actual incident.

My husband had been admitted to the hospital due to an exacerbation of his multiple sclerosis, and had developed a flu-like illness. Part of the diagnostic tests was a chest x-ray. I had been up all night for several nights with him and had been there around the clock at the hospital. I usually never allowed him to be anywhere in the hospital, if at all possible, unless I was right by his side. I felt that since he could not at this time speak, it was necessary for me to be there for communication.

On this day, he was scheduled for the x-ray at approximately 2:00 p.m., and I was very tired. When they came to get him for x-ray, I had dozed off to sleep and was really drowsy when they came. Since he did not have to talk about this, I just allowed him to go without me, which turned out to be almost deadly.

He suffered from apnea, and therefore, when laid flat, sometimes there were problems. Well, when they brought him back to the room, he was lying flat. I did not really notice, but at that point he appeared to be sleeping. When the x-ray tech asked me to plug the bed back in, I did, notating that he was "asleep." I sat back down in the recliner and was about to snooze again when a voice told me to raise the head of the bed. Of course, there was no one there; it was in my head. Guess who was talking?

Well, I got up and raised the head of the bed and straightened the pillow, only to note that my husband was not asleep; he was not breathing. I immediately started to arouse him and tried to get him to breathe, thinking this was an apnea episode that had happened so many times before. When I shook him and he opened his eyes, he tried to breathe, but could not. I shook him again and got the bed up higher. I called the nurse, and no one was coming. I ran into the hall and screamed, "Help! I need help!"

There in the hall was the respiratory therapist, and they came in and we tried to get him to breathe. The therapist called for a crash cart and the nurse who had just come in said, "No, he is a DNR. We cannot resuscitate."

I was frantic trying to get my husband to breathe. I suddenly began to cry out to Jesus, "Tell me what to do, Lord!" With that, the nurse joined me in the cry to Jesus, and then I said, "Check his mouth. See if there is anything in his throat."

With that, the nurse pulled his mouth open, reached in, and pushed his tongue down. Immediately, he gasped for air and once again was breathing. The first response is to check the airway, but when there is an emergency, sometimes the very thing that should be done is the only thing that is not. Today, once again, Jesus came through for us, and once again, my husband was spared for another six years.

Miracles do happen, and happen because we trust and believe that He is able to and will give these to us. I implore you to remember this story and remember to check an airway. Had I not been there, I would have received that old adage, "He just went in his sleep peacefully." Well, that may or may not be the case. Certainly that was not the case this day. God placed me where he intended me to be, because my husband wanted to be here for me as long as he could. I thank my God for the many things He has done for me and is still doing today. He is the God of miracles, and in today's world, we need lots of them. When King David was in despair, he cried out to the Lord. The Lord responded then and this day for me.

I give Him the glory for being the Almighty and only God of miracles.

The Blessed Vision

In early 1996, my Lord anointed me to teach for Him. I have that desire to teach whenever there is a revelation to all who will listen. This was the case with my precious grandson, and I wanted him to have all the resources I could cram into his young spirit. This has continued for all these years, and now, being an adult, sometimes it is difficult for him to still listen to Meemaw's direction.

As a child in his walker, he loved being in the kitchen with me and was always under my feet. He was especially active when in his walker, and I was always afraid he would touch the hot stove when I was baking. I took him over to the stove when it was very warm, but not so hot as to burn him, to teach him it was hot, and warn, "No, no." Well, that became a constant reminder to keep him aware of the danger of the hot oven door.

One day, when I was very busy with my back turned, you guessed it, he went over and touched the hot door and burned blisters on his little hands. I cried with him and hoped his pain would be a lesson to never get near anything hot. I am still trying to keep him from getting burned. I admonish him often about the things I have learned for him to be safe in the hands of a Holy God.

On a Sunday morning not too long ago, I had occasion to meet him and my son and daughter-in-law for brunch. As the time progressed, there was some talk regarding some of God's rules that I felt they were not following. The conversation became a joke to them, and I felt I was being made fun of, but more so that what I was saying about God's Word was being mocked.

Later that day, I sent an email to them and my disappointment that they mocked me and essentially God. My grandson took offense to this, and an altercation began that was very hurtful. I was devastated, to be sure. I had always loved and supported him, as he had me since his birth. I considered him my son and loved him in the same way. His harsh words of unmerited accusation were just too much for me to stand. Emails did not get any better, and eventually I was very hurt. I cried for three days that I could not stop. This was just beyond my understanding. Then, the third day came to a close, and God began.

After much prayer and thought over the circumstances of this, I sat in my chair and I began to ask my Lord for instruction as to scripture He would have me to read and what message He might have me and others who may have suffered like situations. As I sat with my eyes closed, resting and breathing with my Bible on my lap, a most amazing thing occurred.

There in the distance, on the blank slate of my closed eyes, there appeared a small dot of light, which moved closer and closer. It was surrounded by fog, with this reflecting with my eyes closed. It moved to a closeness that I could see it was some sort of a plaque. Then, it moved closer. There, with the fog covering, was what appeared to be an antique plaque. It was an antique cream color with what appeared to be cracks in it and an oval area inside the frame structure with script markings of ribbon design in metallic gold color. On top of these were thin, golden ribbons with antique lace or baby's breath and tiny pink rosebuds entwined in the ribbon. Inside the adorned area was script that looked like calligraphy in a soft black tone. It read, "Cling to me, for I am your God."

As I looked at it in shock, I knew the Lord Himself was speaking to me in comfort and promise that He is with me and that I am His. I felt He was giving me assurance that He will take care of this and whatever I need from Him. What an amazing act of love He afforded me that day!

I wanted to write this down lest my ol' brain forget. The incident was one of a definite vision, and I know that to be true. Even more so, I have the confirmation that I am His, and that is more important than I can ever say.

As I continued to think about this over this week, I felt that the Lord was also saying to me that He has to be number one in my life; that no one, regardless of relationship, can come before Him. I am committed to this, and pray for Him to keep me ever close and never to move away or allow anyone to hold that special place in my heart that rightfully belongs to Him.

A real miracle just for me, but the reassurance it has given to my spirit is worth everything life can bring. I praise Him who is indeed my God, and I love Him as His child.

A Most Precious Soul

"And the king communed with them; and among them all was found none like Daniel."
—Daniel 1:19

I want to introduce you to one of the most precious souls I have ever had the privilege to know. First of all, as I continue here, you may say, "That is a grandma's prejudice," but as I write this introduction, you will sincerely have to admit there is something very special about this young man.

It was very early on a Monday morning that my daughter came to my home to assist me in cleaning. She had three young children and needed some extra money to help take care of some household bills. Not wanting her to leave her children, I chose to hire her to do housework for me while I had the pleasure of spending time with my grandchildren. It worked well for us all.

Today, I noticed something was different, even somewhat wrong. My daughter appeared sad and distant. I questioned her, but she was not ready to release her secret. As the day went on, she was grouchy and seemed to not be into cleaning and certainly not ready to talk. We crossed on several occasions, and then when I thought it just could not go on, she broke and began crying inconsolably. I tried to hold her and be of help, but to no avail. I left her to make her own choice as to when she wanted to talk.

After a couple of hours of silence, we were beginning to clean the kitchen when she blurted out, "I'm pregnant." It stopped me in my tracks, for sure, since my granddaughter, who was the youngest of three, was around fifteen months old, and my son-in-law had undergone a vasectomy to be sure there were no more children. She shared that her husband, having had a vasectomy right after their daughter was born, failed to get the confirmation test, and now he would be livid that she was possibly pregnant.

As we talked, I knew that the marriage was stressed and money problems would become worse with another child to feed. She was afraid to tell him. How could this be possible? Would he even accept it at all? I suggested that she call the doctor for an appointment and to tell her husband as soon as possible. She accepted my advice and did as I said.

When she came the next morning, she was somewhat relieved but angry at her husband. He, while knowing that she had been faithful only to him, was very upset at what was going on. Though he knew her well, that little bit of doubt was creeping into his understanding, and that became a real problem. So, his solution was insisting that she have an abortion. Of course, I exploded at the thought. Then, we had words. She was angry at him, but she was more angry with me for ridiculing him. She had every explanation of why they could not afford another child, and too, her in-laws were pro-choice people and felt she should consider their situation as a family, not as a Godly thing.

Days went by, and stress became more and more, and it was almost impossible for us to be together. I, being a dedicated Christian, would in no way condone the thought of abortion. She was fighting for her marriage, because her husband insisted, "It is that thing in you, or me?" He had made it quite clear if she chose to have this baby, he was leaving her. What a mess!

Then, you have to consider what he was going through: believing in his heart that his wife was faithful and true, but with his scientific mind telling him this was not possible and something had to be wrong here. He dealt with this as well as he could, but nine months after a vasectomy? She was truly afraid he was going to leave, and how could she support the three precious little ones she had and go through delivery of another child? This was a real problem, and one that only God could solve.

My sister came up from Florida for the summer. She, being a dedicated Christian and a favorite person to my daughter, had to help me. As she talked to my daughter, she related to me that this poor, precious girl was really in a mess. She adored her husband, and of course she was not the only one involved here. She was no more at fault than was he, but she had to shoulder the blame. My sister offered to go with her to her doctor's appointment, and I kept the other children. Her husband felt she would make the abortion appointment, and I was on my knees to God to please do something. I knew full well that the obstetrician would not do an abortion, but he could recommend one if she insisted.

As I prayed, my sister went into the exam room with her and then into the consultation that followed. She and her aunt decided that she would tell her husband that she was too far along for an abortion and take the consequences. The same story was told to me and to the in-laws, and so we were safe in a sort of lie. I truly believed that we had a miracle and that the baby was saved by God. It was many years later before I learned the truth.

So, on September 15, 2001, a real miracle happened: that of the birth of this special child. He was perfect in every way, beautiful and loving. His name was chosen from the Word of God, Daniel, because he was being thrown into a lion's den, for sure.

Much stress followed in the marriage; however, her husband did not physically leave. He was spiritually absent to her and rarely touched the new son, though he was the image of his dad. He rejected this child all his life, and until only in the recent year has he shown him any affection whatsoever. The marriage failed due to reasons we will not go into here, and Daniel became his Meemaw's real pride and joy. He was, from the beginning, a child who was the first to run and hug you, and he gained favor from everyone who came in contact with him.

He said to me, "The Book of Daniel is my book because it is my name." I was surprised that his dad allowed him to be named Daniel. Jenna has tried to choose biblical names for her children. Daniel fits this young man even more than expected for what he has gone through.

Now, to tell you about Daniel. What a mess he was and a bundle of energy, as well as a bundle of joy. I took him to Sunday school, where he won the hearts of all who had the occasion to spend time with him. But, then another trait came forth: his Sunday school teacher came to me to compliment me for teaching him the Bible. While that was certainly refreshing to know, I had not really been teaching him the Bible. The teacher shared that he would give details to the Sunday school lesson, as if he had been taught it completely and explicitly. I noticed, as well, that he had an unusual, simple knowledge that was unexplainable.

Then came his compassion to the elderly and to anyone who was afflicted. It seemed he was drawn to people who were wheelchair bound, or on crutches, or mentally afflicted. He just could not stay away from them. He just wanted to give them a hug and hold their hands. The elderly in the church waited for him to come give them a hug. The people of the church took turns having Daniel sit with them during church, and I would question him about the sermon on the way home. Even though he would be busy doing a puzzle or coloring, he heard every word. Also, when the pastor called for anyone who wanted to come to the altar for prayer, Daniel was there behind the altar rail with the pastor. The pastor told me, "God has a call on this child's life."

Daniel was a helper. He wanted to help with everything. Whenever we had a special occasion at the church, he was the first to want to help set up tables and clean up afterward, and was excited to sit and talk to any of the elders one on one. The elders commented that this young man had wisdom beyond his years.

He was now old enough to start school. Once again, Daniel showed that he was special when introduced to a young, quite frightened girl with Down's syndrome, and he immediately calmed her down. Daniel would take her hand and lead her to class, and she would look for him. Her mother was thrilled at Daniel's attention to Zana, and this friendship continued through school and is still present today.

When Merit Day came at the end of the year, Daniel received an award for his friendship and help to other students. Daniel hugs everyone, male and female alike, and was never embarrassed to give a holy kiss on the forehead to everyone. This practice is done at our church, and Daniel loves to show everyone he meets this kind of love.

Several weeks ago, we were in church when an older lady came down the aisle to be seated. She walked on two crutches, much like people who had polio in the forties, as I remember. When Daniel saw her, he, without hesitation, jumped up from his seat to escort her and assist with seating her. When church was over, he immediately left his friends to assist this stranger to her car. This was one act of many, and he loves doing what he can to help others.

Our pastor asked him to be a mentor to a slightly mentally disabled young man at camp one summer two years ago. His parents complimented him on making the camp special for their child. Daniel did a good job, being responsible and personable to that young boy, who, if not for Daniel, might have not been allowed to attend camp.

He is responsible in work ethics. A neighbor pays Daniel to care for her animals when she is out of town. He treats this as a job, and she pays him very well for doing this. When he gets paid, he keeps just a few dollars and gives the rest to his mom to help with household needs. Many times I have seen him give part of his money to his brother, just because his brother did not have any. He will share everything with his siblings. I have felt he was taken advantage of, but he says no, he wants to share with them. I have had the occasion to take him out to eat, and he wants me to get something to take home for them. Always thinking of others, loving them and serving them.

One day, he threw up at school, so I picked him up, and on the way home we stopped by Walmart to get something. When we got out of the car, we saw a lady in a handicap cart with lots of groceries waiting in front. I thought he was with me, but when I turned around, he was not there. I walked back to the door, and there he was, helping the lady get into the waiting car and assisting with her groceries. He came in and apologized, saying, "Sorry, Meemaw, but that lady needed help." God placed another mark on his list of good works for Daniel.

There are so many episodes like this with Daniel that I will write down later when I remember them, but Daniel feels he has been called into a special field of service: that of being a teacher of special-needs children. He is being taught by God in this endeavor. He has kept his grades high and is accepting training as the Lord would have him to receive. This training is sometimes difficult to swallow, given the loving person that Daniel is, but nevertheless, the training is necessary for his upcoming call.

Just before leaving middle school, Daniel had a difficult problem that evolved from his love of everyone and wanting to show affection to all. A very crude misunderstanding took place, in which he was accused of breaking the school rule of "no touching." This accusation came as he hugged his best friend and gave him a kiss on the forehead. You can just guess what he was accused of, and this was devastating to this loving youngster. He served a penalty of having to be in class alone for several days, but the accusation was almost more than Daniel could take. He was literally sick, throwing up at the thought, and when we picked him up from school, a very dejected kid was seen.

We took him out to eat and did not talk about the episode called "sexual abuse," but rather talked about the strong lesson he received from a loving God. After I explained that as a special-needs teacher, he would have to hold back hugs, etc., and that needed to be accepted by him now, he said he understood and counted it as a blessing. The mother of his best friend was livid that such a thing had happened when the boys had been friends so long. She defended Daniel to the school and put on record her total disagreement to the punishment and assessment by the school officials.

Daniel held his head high when back in class, but was careful to not hug or show affection to anyone else. It has taken real strength to change his actions, but as I explained to him, he is now a young man. He needs to watch his actions, which will be important as he matures into manhood. He has conquered that and matured as the Lord continues to lead him. He has been accepted by the older teens, as well, now, and shares friendships with many of them as really close friends.

He was so excited to go on his class trip to Charleston, South Carolina. When I asked him to tell about the trip, his only real excitement was a homeless man named John, whom he gave his leftover food and his time for a conversation. It broke Daniel's heart to hear his life story and his descent into poverty, but it was definitely a story that was intended for Daniel to hear.

Daniel finished middle school with good grades and a good outlook for his upper-class years. I advised him to keep his grades high, and I check with them often so as to encourage high grades for hopes of getting a scholarship for his chosen vocation.

A short time ago, our pastor called Daniel and asked if he would like to go to lunch with him. Pastor Ed, a long-time youth director, before becoming our pastor, has been watching Daniel as he is maturing. Daniel said that Pastor Ed wanted to compliment his growth in his Christian faith and in his maturity with the group. He talked to him regarding his plans for the future, which Daniel shared what he felt the Lord was calling him to. Pastor Ed asked if he had considered being a pastor, that he felt Daniel was showing great signs of leadership and possible ministry. Daniel was quite pleased at the confidence that was shown to him, and is praying for complete light in the direction the Lord has for him. God chose Daniel to be born, and to the ones to whom He gave this miracle, He is in control here.

Daniel has not changed his mind about what he feels the Lord would have him to do. He is still helping others and still adamant of his calling to be a special-needs teacher. He is working hard to maintain his high grade average, and has chosen to go to a local college. Daniel is a most precious soul. He is not only a miracle child, but a complete joy to all who know him. I am sure if you have the opportunity to meet this young man, you will certainly agree.

If this gives you a small picture of my grandson, perhaps you will be blessed someday to recall an incident that you, too, witnessed one of Daniel's astonishing acts. Watch for miracles in regard to him. God has him in the palm of His hand, for he is indeed a most special soul.

Confident

"Being confident of this very thing, that he which hath begun a good work in you will perform it until the day of Jesus Christ."
—*Philippians: 1:6*
"Let us therefore come boldly unto the throne of grace, that we may obtain mercy, and find grace to help in time of need."
—*Hebrews 4:16*

It was October 22, 2011, that I became Mrs. Roger Boykin and began a new life with a most amazing man. Our life was cut short when he suffered a stroke that would lead to eight months of bedridden illness unto his death July 22, 2017.

Roger had accepted Christ about a month before our marriage, and had interacted with me in Bible studies and church activities. However, he was having mini strokes all along that would cause him to eventually pull away from these things. Roger had lost his way. With his illness so serious now, I was concerned for his soul. I tried to talk to him about it to no avail, and even hostility, and I was becoming very frustrated. It appeared he was also pulling away from me.

A severe infection in a diabetic lesion on his foot led to another hospitalization that revealed a very low blood count, and because of previous transfusion, blood was not available, nor could it be matched. He was declining rapidly. I knew I could not care for him at home anymore, and so he was admitted to a convalescent home for possible therapy and care. We had been there previously for therapy when he first had the stroke, so he felt comfortable there and knew the caretakers.

On that first day we moved into the room, many of the other patients who remembered him, and nurses, and caregivers came by to welcome him. He was "at home." Then, a strange thing happened. As we were there alone in the room, the door opened, and in came a little white-haired old lady in a wheelchair. Rolled right into the room. Angrily, she yelled at Roger, "You get out of my house, and don't you come back! If you do, I will get a bulldozer and throw your ass out the window!"

Roger looked questionably in shock and a bit scared. I told her, "This is not your house. This is his room, and you get out." With that, I pushed her chair out and closed the door.

That night, Roger's blood again dropped and he went into a coma for a period, and they wanted to send him back to the hospital. I knew they would only send him home and I would be in a no-win situation. I begged the people and doctor to keep him. They agreed only if I signed a DNR, which I did.

His daughter came, and he rallied quite miraculously. Time went on through the early summer, and he began to decline again with kidney malfunction and liver failing. It appeared all systems were breaking down. The doctor called me aside and told me that his bone marrow was not producing blood cells, and he was dying. I was devastated, but upon knowing this, I asked that all medication be stopped and only feeding him through the peg tube. I was sick at heart, but still praying for his return to the Lord.

On Sunday I came to the facility, as I usually did. We listened to some of the Sunday ministers who were on TV. We both were so tired that he and I dozed off to sleep. I was awakened with the same little old lady touching me. She said, "Are you all right, honey?" I told her I was tired. With that, she laid her hand on me and began to pray. As she prayed, she sobbed and was very emotional in a most fervent prayer for my peace. She then said, "Amen," and pointing to Roger, asked, "How is he doing?" I just shook my head. She then rolled over to the bed, where Roger opened his eyes and smiled at her. She took his hand and asked, "Do you love Jesus?"

Roger shook his head yes. She said, "Don't shake your head. Speak to me. Answer me so He can hear you. Do you love Jesus?"

Roger said, "Yes."

She smiled and told him, "You see, when He hears you say you love Him, He will take care of you. Do you know that?"

Roger began to cry and his lips quivered, as he was saying yes. With that, she began to pray an intercessional prayer like none I have ever heard, sobbing for his spirit to be lifted and filled, and that a Holy God would be forgiving, and restoring, and healing. After a prayer with the Holy Spirit so strong you could feel it all over the room, she said, "Believe." She then exited the room.

I got up to wipe Roger's tears, and he took my hand and said, "Confident."

I said, "What?"

He said, "I am confident." Roger was back. He had made his peace with the Lord and now was ready to face whatever comes with confidence.

Roger went to be with the Lord just one week later. A miracle had been given to us through a most unlikely source—nevertheless the miracle we needed for Roger to be taken into the presence of the Lord.

The Lord giveth and the Lord taketh away. Thanks be to Him for his miracles.

$\mathcal{D}$on't Use That Saw!

"But the Comforter, which is the Holy Ghost, whom the Father will send in my name, he shall teach you all things, and bring all things to your remembrance, whatsoever I have said unto you."
—John 14:26

I t was about 1996, when I was called to teach, that I chose to attend a ladies' Bible study. A monthly plan was for each member of your group to host lunch at their personal home when it was your turn. My time would be coming soon, and my house was just not appropriate to have people to come there, so I began some needed renovations. One of the things was to open up the wall between my living room and dining area. Thus began "Roni Toolbox." I decided I could do all of this myself. Of course, I had to have the help of the Lord. Understand, I did this when Richard was at work, so he would not stop me. So, here I go, diving right in.

This particular day, I had marked the wall to be removed and drew the picture on the wall to be cut. I promptly went into the utility room and got my husband's skill saw, and readied to begin. Just as I placed the saw on the line to be cut, that voice I know so well advised, "Don't use that saw." Once again, I got set, and again, "Don't use that saw."

So, I unplugged the saw and changed to the saber saw, which had a blade just long enough to go through the sheetrock, and proceeded to cut. As I completed the cut out, I removed the piece of sheetrock, and to my surprise and gratitude, I saw what my Lord knew would have been very dangerous. There, running through the wall, was the large electric wire that supplied the socket I was plugged into. The skill saw would have indeed cut right through the wire, and I would be glowing, if there at all!

The Holy Spirit warned me so as to keep me safe, and because I listened, I was spared the consequences of possible electrical shock. Believe me, when I saw this, I shook all over just to think how close I was to being hurt.

I had this big wire running through the hole where I wanted to open the wall completely. So, what do I do about this? Kelli said, "My friend works with an electrician. Let's call him."

So, we called, and were informed to "just pull it out." We were also told to first turn off the breaker in the electrical box. So, we turned off the breaker, detached the wire from the socket it was tied into, and pulled the wire out. All done! You think?

We proceeded to smooth the areas where the wall had been, and then we knocked out the three 2 x 4s in the middle, we being my sister and partner in crime and me, and let's not forget, the Lord. So proud of what we had accomplished, but we did have to use the skill saw to saw the one 2 x 4 on the floor to remove it.

This day's work was done, and we cleaned up the mess, and Joyce went home until the next day. I went into the den, which was next to these two rooms, and turned on the television for a spell. Did I say "turned on"? Actually, the television would not come on, nor would the lamps. No power in the room. I had detached the electrical source.

It was about dinnertime, so I went into the kitchen to make food to be ready when Richard got home from work, which was shortly. When he arrived, he observed my work effort and complimented me, and was really impressed. Then, I told him there was no power in the den. I said, "Can you help me fix it?"

He did not shout or ridicule me at all. He only said, "You did it. You fix it."

So, the next day's chore was certainly set. "Now, Lord, show me how to do this."

Joyce arrived about 10:30 a.m., and we enjoyed coffee and laughed about our mess. We also began to confer regarding where to begin and how.

That wire I pulled out had to be rejoined to an electrical source, that being another socket. Miraculously, after I climbed into the attic and drilled several misplaced holes, we found the right place to pull the wire through and attach it to another outlet that produced power, and we were back in business. Now, to close the holes that were drilled in the wrong place.

God was indeed my coach that day, and gave me the miracle of His presence to teach me a very great lesson: the miracle of listening. We finished the door and it looked pretty good, but then I was on a roll and next project was at hand.

The Holy Spirit will always be there to speak to you in times like this, but we must also be ready to listen for His warning. Miracles happen in just everyday things we do when we are willing to listen and trust. Truly, "He will teach you all things."

The Rose

*"The wilderness and the solitary place shall be glad for them;
and the desert shall rejoice, and blossom as the rose."*
—*Isaiah 35:1*

Today is October 11, 2010. Today I begin a new era of my life. All things to this day are complete, and now I await direction to open a new path in which God will lead me through the end of my life. This is a new day in which I give Him full charge of what I am to do, where I am to walk, and with whom I will spend these latter days. As I go into the seventy-fifth year, it seems unbelievable that I have lived seventy-four years and come this far. Yet more unbelievable: that He has chosen me to be His child. I am so blessed to have had the life I have, the family I have, and the love I have from Him.

The past year had been a difficult one. The economy had thrown a monkey wrench into the lives of everyone I know, especially in my family. I had felt very alone at times and felt left out of so many events. I was doing everything I possibly could do to help, and now I found myself in a pinch, and concern was setting in. I felt that there was no one to turn to, not even anyone to talk to for comfort. But, then there was my God. He was always there, always bringing the necessary to help me through the circumstances which led to my sadness.

September 20 was one of those days. I was having myself a pity party and once again not remembering how blessed I am. This was my deceased husband's birthday. My children wanted to go to the cemetery and take flowers, but I did not want to go. I was feeling the loss that day, remembering the past and the one who had loved me so much. I became pretty adamant as I told the girls that their daddy was not in that piece of ground. I refused to go and look at the dirt and pretend that he was still there. Richard was in Heaven with my God.

As the day pressed on, my guilt got the best of me. I cried and asked God to forgive my harshness, and I also spoke aloud to Richard, apologizing to him. I remembered that even on his birthday, I was given a red rose. It seemed that Richard would sense when I was a little down, and he would come with one long-stemmed red rose for me. Even when he was so very ill and bedridden, he would manage to get one of the children to go buy me a red rose, whether a special occasion or just because. The red rose was always special to me; I was always special to Richard. He not only believed the scripture "Husbands, love your wives, even as Christ also loved the church," (Ephesians 5:25), but he lived it every day of our marriage. He was "true blue," so to speak—always faithful to me, always obedient to his God.

I had not so long ago accidentally driven through my garage and spoiled my prayer garden. As a result of rebuilding, I planted rosebushes there. One was a beautiful red one, one a soft pink, and one nearly-white climbing rose for an arbor. I placed a fountain, and a bench separated the bushes, along with other little items to make it more appealing. Several times a week I went into the garden and pinched the spent blooms off the rosebushes and added water to keep them hydrated well. I noticed several days before that there were many new buds going through their process of maturity, but one bud on the soft-pink bush seemed to be a little darker in color than the rest. I wondered about it, but gave no specific attention to it.

The garden is right outside a large picture window in my dining area and is always a beautiful scene to behold. The afternoon sun comes in so very brightly that it is necessary to close the blinds to protect the table, etc. As I went to look out the large picture window and to adjust the blinds, much to my surprise, a real unusual phenomenon came into view. I could hardly believe my eyes as I beheld the glory of my God's creation right outside my window. There in my prayer garden, on the pink rose bush, was one red rose. Today, on Richard's birthday, during my sadness, one red rose on the same stem with two pink roses—how could this be?

You and others may say that there was cross pollination, and perhaps so, but in the presentation of one solid red rose, and on the same stem with two pink ones, and the rest of the bush all pink? I choose not to accept this as a coincidence, but rather a direct gift from God. My God knows my every thought and every hurt, and finds a way to dry my tears. Although many tears flowed that day when I saw this, they were tears of joy. A feeling of so much love encompassed me that I felt I had to share this with everyone I know. How very special I felt at that time. How very special indeed was this gesture from my God—not because I deserved it, nor because I am more special than anyone else, but just because my God is all knowing and all present and all powerful.

My Lord chose to show me once again the love that had been given to me through a most special man, my husband, and his practice all those years. You see, God is a romantic, too. He is everything I need, exactly when I need it, always faithful. God gave me one red rose confirming my belief that Richard was indeed there with Him. Confirmation that I, too, will one day join Him there. "Absent from the body, and to be present with the Lord."

The special love He supplied me through Richard was only an extension of the great love He has for me, in that He gave His only son to die on the cross that I, Revonda, may have eternal life. Psalms 139 says, "Thou knowest my downsitting and mine uprising, thou understandest my thought afar off. Thou compassest my path and my lying down, and art acquainted with all my ways." God knows.

As amazing as was the one rose on with two pink roses, same stem, another quite miraculous rose appeared to me. This time was during a drastic move in the life of my second marriage to a most special man. This was a time when I had been very busy making renovations to my daughter's home. I had not given the time nor respect to my then-husband Roger, and feeling slighted, he was showing interest in another. I suffered through this, and the Lord took care of it in a way that only He can do, but then He let me know He was with me with another special rose on the pink bush. This rose was all pink except for one petal that was red and in the perfect shape of a heart. How could the Lord do even a greater miracle to show that He was with me and loved me? That rose I have chosen to be on the cover of this and any other book I may write because it is special, so special, and yet not impossible for my God.

Miracles like this rose are ordinary for Him and there for everyone who chooses to believe and look for them. God is no respecter of persons, and therefore, what is done for me is certainly there to be done for you. Look for His hand in your life. There are miracles galor---ious every day you choose to receive them.

About the Author

Revonda Lee Gregg was born in Marietta, Georgia, in 1936. Living in this small town, which grew to a metropolis seemingly overnight, brought her wonderful experiences, of which she witnessed and began to document. Her marriage to Richard Zubiena in the late 1960s enhanced her life with three children, Kelli, Scot, and Jenna. Six grandchildren have completed her joy. After forty-eight years of marriage, Richard succumbed from a long illness.

Now living in North Georgia, she married Roger Boykin, who brought her much happiness for a short six years. After his death, Revonda chose to put the miracles she had been given into this book, which is now published to the glory of God.